© 2025 ELLIS POTTER

Without limiting the rights under copyright reserved above, no part of this publication may be reproduced, stored in, or introduced into a retrieval system, or transmitted in any form or by any means (electronic, mechanical, photocopying, or otherwise), without the prior written permission from the publisher, except where permitted by law, and except in the case of brief quotations embodied in critical articles and reviews. For information, write: info@destineemedia.com
Reasonable care has been taken to trace original sources and copyright holders for any quotations appearing in this book. Should any attribution be found to be incorrect or incomplete, the publisher welcomes written documentation supporting correction for subsequent printing.

Published by: Destinée Media
www.destineemedia.com

Cover design by Ben Stone
Cover and interior by Ben Stone
Formatting by Ben Stone

All rights reserved by the author.
ISBN 978-1-938367-85-4

Christian Thoughts for Weekdays

Ellis Potter

Introduction

This book of 260 devotional thoughts is made up of Pastor Potter's Points vol. I and II plus 60 more. Each thought is only 100 words and short enough to be used on busy weekdays. On the weekends you can read other, longer things. Some people use the thoughts as mealtime devotionals, which can start good conversations. The thoughts are arranged randomly rather than thematically or alphabetically so they change the subject each day. To give you an idea of the length of the thoughts this introduction is also 100 words. May God bless you through these short thoughts.

- Ellis Potter
Basel, 2025

Week One

Monday

Bible Principles and Applications

Many people ask if the Bible is "relevant" today. The principles of the Bible are eternally true. The applications of the principles are culturally specific. For instance, Jesus taught His disciples to wash each other's feet. The principle behind this is humble, practical daily service. In most Churches today foot washing has been reduced to an annual ceremony, so the principle is lost. A better application today would be "wash each other's dishes.". We should not ask how the Bible is relevant to our culture but how our culture is relevant to the Bible. Don't fit the Bible into your life. Fit your life into the Bible.

Tuesday

Holy Selfishness

The couple decided to be more generous with their time, money, caring and praying. They gave more without expecting to be repaid. Then they discovered that their lives, peace and wellbeing increased. With God, you can't really give things away because they come back to you as blessings, seen and unseen, present and eternal. When we invest in the Kingdom of God, we are in-vesting in ourselves with a certainty of a rich return. Those we bless become part of a rich crown of reward for us. When we are un-selfish, God establishes our selves for us.

Wednesday

Baptism Testimony

I believe that God; Father, Son and Holy Spirit, has made the world and me and I did not make myself.

I have rebelled against God and tried to make myself according to my ideas and desires. This self-creation cannot be sustained and so it is dead.

I believe Jesus Christ has come into the world and died on the cross so I might have life again.

I have accepted this new life with thanks and am resolved to live as God intends me to live with His help.

Thursday

Art

Art is artificial, made by the arm of people. Natural things and events can be very pleasing and inspiring, but they are never art. Art is Deliberate Human Action and is responsible. Art is what people do with nature in agriculture, painting, music, cooking, dancing, architectture, etc. Art is responsible dominion over nature. Art is expressions and statements by people. The point is what they say, not whether we like it. Art is not for consumption but for relationships and dialogue. We dehumanize art when we commodify it. Art is not about me but about us. Join the conversation.

Friday

Assurance of Salvation

People who belong to God through Jesus Christ are saved and secure even if they are crippled physically or psychologyically. Salvation does not depend on what we feel about Jesus but on what He has done for us and His power to keep us. Our mood or physical condition is not a good measure of our relationship with God and our growth as His child. A better measure is whether we are growing or shrinking in the fruits of the Spirit: Love, Joy, Peace, Patience, Kindness, Goodness, Faithfulness, Gentleness and Self-Control. May God protect us from being discouraged by our discouragements. Amen.

Week Two

Monday

The Power of Prayer

The power of prayer is to develop the relationship between us and God and us and those we pray with. This is permanent and eternal. Prayer brings about specific miracles of health, weather, political outcomes, jobs, exams, spouses and parking places. These are all temporary. Everyone who has been miraculously healed has died later. It is important to ask God about everything. He gives us what He knows will bless us. A man doesn't give his boy a motorcycle if he knows he will kill himself with it. Pray in the Name and Will of Jesus.

Tuesday

Christian Listening and Reading

Christians have sometimes been careless readers and listeners from the very beginning. In John 21:22-23 Jesus asked Peter what difference it would make to him if John never died until Jesus returned. People began to say John would never die. It is exciting and dramatic to say this kind of thing, but it can lead to confusion, disappointment, and tensions. Take care to read and hear what is actually there rather than what gives a thrill or proves your point. God help us to be humble and disciplined in our reading, hearing, and speaking. Amen.

Wednesday

Citizenship in Heaven

They told the little boy there was a present for him, kept high up in the closet. On his birthday he will not climb up in the closet to get it. It will be brought to him. Our citizenship is kept for us in heaven. We will not go to heaven to get it. When Jesus appears and God's Kingdom comes, He will bring it to us here on earth. God's Kingdom is His Will. We should live so that His Kingdom comes in our hearts, lives and relationships more and more each day while we wait.

Thursday

Apologetics as Love

People need to know the Gospel is the only fully rational and accurate way to understand reality. More deeply they need to be freed from blindness and able to see their own sin and need for God. Our apologetics should be motivated by love and aim at encouraging people toward this freedom. May God help us be prepared to give an answer and soften our hearts to love those we answer. Amen.

Friday

Post Modern Beatitudes

1. Blessed are the self-confident for they will succeed.
2. Blessed are those who avoid guilt feelings for they are comforted.
3. Blessed are those with a positive selfimage for they will feel better.
4. Blessed are those who clarify their values for they will invent themselves.
5. Blessed are those who know their rights for they will realize their entitlements.
6. Blessed are those who are non-stick surfaced for they will be admired.
7. Blessed are those who mob and gossip for they will move forward.
8. Blessed are those who are politically correct for they will avoid controversy.

Week Three

Monday

Restrictions

More and more, people are offended by restrictions and claim increasing freedom in life, especially in identifying themselves. When someone gets the freedom to drive a car they must learn and observe many strong restrictions. Freedom from the restrictions will cause death to the driver and others. Freedom to use human language requires submitting to many restrictions or communication will not happen. Restrictions shape the lively truth of our freedoms. God gives us many restrictions in the Bible. These are not for making life smaller but for making life possible and clearly defined. Accept God's restrictions and live.

Tuesday

Confession

Confessing our sins, specific and general, and getting God's forgiveness and cleansing are essential for the Christian life. Remember each day to bring your sins, known and unknown, to God for forgiveness and cleansing by the blood of Jesus. This clears out the clogging garbage of our lives and gives us a fresh start. It makes us more able to receive God's blessing, guidance and empowerment to serve and bless others. When God has forgiven you, forgive yourself and move on. Don't hang on to false guilt. Make this a daily habit, alone or with others.

Wednesday

Cool

Cool communication is emotional and experiential and does not invite discussion. It is neither true nor false – just cool. Cool expresses taste, which is not debatable. (de gustibus non est disputandum). Cool flies beneath the radar of logic and invites participation without decision making or commitment. It is useful for advertising and ropaganda. Hot communication contains content that is definite, committed and either true or false. It invites discussion and decision making. The Gospel of Jesus Christ is hot communication, presenting categories of reality that are either right or wrong and invite a decision. Jesus is not cool.

Thursday

What is in a Name?

A Name is not just a label. A name is a character or reputation. "They have a good name." Or "They have a bad name". When we pray in the Name of Jesus, we don't just tack a signature onto the end of our prayer to give it authenticity. The Name of Jesus is His Character. Our prayers must be in the Character of Jesus in order to be acceptable and effective. His Character includes His Will. We must pray in His Will, not only our own. "In Jesus' Name" includes "If it be Your Will."

Friday

Authenticity

Authentic means genuine or honest. More deeply it means coming from the self as in autograph or autobiography. Only God comes from Himself. Everyone and everything else begins with God and not the self. If anything or anyone is "self-referential" it has no meaning because meaning means relationships. Since God is the SELF that causes everything there is no true meaning except in relation to Him. May God help us to take off the pressure to invent ourselves and put it on Jesus, Who can bear it and deal with it perfectly. Amen. Receive your true self from Jesus.

Week Four

Monday

Guilt and Hope

Without guilt there is no hope. Guilt is very unpopular and politically incorrect in our days. People are encouraged to ignore and suppress their feelings of guilt. This might give some relief. If we are not guilty, we are only innocent victims of our circumstances and need to be compensated, understood, accepted and tolerated. People might promise to do that, but no one is able. If we are guilty, we need to be forgiven and restored. Someone is promising to do that. If we bring our broken selves to God through Jesus Christ, we have true hope for the future.

Tuesday

Evil

Good and evil are not equal opposites. Good is original and evil is a distortion or counterfeit. Evil cannot exist without good but good exists without evil. Evil appears in ways we fear and hate. Evil is more dangerous when it is attractive to us. Evil attracts us to participate in it and take it inside ourselves, so we become evil. Evil is rejecting what God gives us and trying to invent ourselves according to our own imagination. Evil was defeated and swallowed up in victory on the Cross. Lead us not into temptation but deliver us from evil.

Wednesday

God is Love

It is important not to think or say, "Love is God". That will lead us to worship whatever impermanent idea or experience we consider love. Love cannot be separated from Truth or Justice. Love is not an emotion but a series of actions that encourage and support the beloved in being who God wants them to be. Love can be gentle or violent, encouraging or rebuking. Love must be free to work independently from our feelings. If we act in love and prayerfully our feelings will come into focus. We need God to teach us how to love.

Thursday

Felt Needs

Many pastors have been taught to preach to the "felt needs" of the people. They are naturally more popular if they do that. Should we expect people's feelings to correspond to what they actually need in God's Kingdom? Or, should we look into the Bible to find out what God says people need? The first approach is natural. The second approach is spiritual. We don't need an us shaped Jesus. We need a Jesus shaped us. God, help us to want what You want. Amen.

Friday

Generational Cursing

Some people have a cloud on their hearts because a grandparent was a witch or a murderer. They think of Exodus 20:5: "…punishing the children for the sin of the fathers to the third and fourth generation.". They miss the last words "of those who hate me.". The question is not what your ancestors did but whether you love the Lord. The consequences of sins (poverty, bad name, ruined ecology) pass on to future generations, but not the guilt. Ezekiel Chapter 18 is full of clarity and comfort on this subject. God help us to live by Your mercy. Amen.

Week Five

Monday

Extra Commandments

Thou Shalt have fun – spectacle

Thou Shalt let it all hang out

Thou Shalt go with the flow

Thou Shalt express Thyself

Thou Shalt have a good self-image

Thou Shalt go for the gusto

Thou Shalt be happy

Thou Shalt get in touch with Thy feelings

Thou Shalt be Natural

Tuesday

Glory

Glory means weight, solid foundation, dependable. It also means radiant and shining. God is Love. Love is the foundation of all reality and everything has meaning in Love. The Glory of God is Love. We should tell God that He is Glorious, proclaim it to the world and sing about it. When we grow in Love for each other and for the needy world, we show God's Love and magnify His Name. We participate in the coming of His Kingdom here on earth. "Your Kingdom come your Will be done, on earth as it is in heaven." Amen.

Wednesday

Confidence and Trust

In times of crises and stress like the Coronavirus pandemic of 2020, it is hard to trust. Governments make mistakes, anyone we meet might infect us, those who control our online life have various agendas. We cannot see or understand all details. But we can see the big picture in God's Person and promises. He promises to keep us so nothing can separate us from Him. All the confusing and stressful details of our lives have their true meaning in the perspective of God's eternal promises. Keep your eyes on Jesus. Think about His power and faithfulness and be at peace.

Thursday

God alone is God and God is not alone

This is only true of the God of the Bible. Buddha alone is Buddha…. Krishna alone is Krishna…. Allah alone is Allah…. All are alone in the beginning. The Christian God is authentically a God of love and relationships because He is three Persons eternally. God is three Persons. The devil is one person. Three persons are other centered. One person is necessarily self-centered as there is no other. One is imploding and dead. Three is radiant and alive. Choose the living God of the Bible for life and love forever.

Friday

God is Green

Many people think God is brown, preparing to burn up His creation and not caring about it in the meantime. The "end" is near, in English, can mean the termination is near or the goal is near. In Greek "telos" only means goal. The goal is the cleansing and renewing of creation, not its destruction. "The end is near" actually means "the beginning is near.". God gave humans the power to take care of His creation, not to exploit it and damage it. Christians and green people need to learn that no one is greener than God.

Week Six

Monday

Godly Sorrow and Mourning

Godly sorrow involves repentance and leads to change. It is sorrow that we are not living our life as God wants us to, which we could do. There are elements of joy and thankfulness in it. Worldly sorrow happens to everyone and might lead nowhere. Godly sorrow is a gift and leads to life. "Blessed are those who mourn" is about those who mourn for their sins and the evil in the world, who are sad because they have offended God. It is about Christians in the Kingdom of God, not about any person who grieves over loss or suffering.

Tuesday

Growing Pains

Is there growth of any kind without pain? When we grow physically, emotionally, intellectually, socially or in holiness the old us dies and the new us comes into being. The old us is familiar. The new us is unknown so we don't know what we will be like. We need to walk by faith in the dark, so we need to take the hand of Jesus and trust the light of Scripture. When you have pain, look for the area of growth. If you find it some pain will remain, but it will have meaning and purpose.

Wednesday

Healing

Healing is a feature of Christianity in the Bible and through the history of the Church. We are all broken and sick and God wants to heal our bodies, our emotions, our minds and our attitudes. Physical healing is a part of our total healing that will happen when Jesus appears. If our bodies are healed and our hearts are not, we lose. If our hearts are healed and our bodies are not, we win. Physical healing is a patch up job because we will die eventually. Healing of our hearts is permanent and eternal.

Thursday

Cups of Cold Water

Giving a cup of cold water to a little one in Jesus brings rewards. Little ones are around us always, especially when people's lives are reduced and isolated. There are many kinds of cups of cold water: an email, a phone call, an encouragement, shopping, a visit or help with the budget so as to have more control over finances in uncertain times. The Lord will show you what kinds of cups are yours to give. Give as many as possible with joy and invest in your eternal treasure and crown. You will be glad forever.

Friday

Hiding from God

Adam and Eve hid from God among the trees of the garden. People hide from the Creator in the creation behind science or evolution. People hide from God in their pride or their entitlements or their victimhood. People believe they know about good and evil from themselves and can declare themselves innocent. We who believe in Jesus can also hide from Him in a mistrusting cover up of shame. When we hide, we cannot be forgiven, healed and transformed. Let us be transparent with God and trust Him completely. Our only true hiding place is actually God.

Week Seven

Monday

Reality II

Reality is Who God is, What He does and What He wants. God is the original reality. He made the universe, which is also real. He made you and me and we are real in His original design and desire. We become unreal by turning away from God and refusing to accept the saving and sustaining of our reality by Him. The devil became unreal through rebellion and tries to draw us into his unreality.

Sin, distortion, sickness, alienation and death are all unrealities that war against us to destroy us. Turn to Jesus and get real!

Tuesday

Leaders and Followers

In the Evangelical world there is a great emphasis on leadership with many books and conferences about it. There are always, of course, more followers than leaders. The quality of the followers is at least as important as the quality of the leaders. Followers should support and encourage leaders, expect much and complain little, test everything, pray for the leaders, avoid gossip like the plague, respond to teaching so the leaders are encouraged to teach better, pray and work to be part of the solution rather than part of the problem. Each follower is needed and important. May God help all followers to take their role seriously. Amen.

Wednesday

Naturalism

Naturalism is the belief that only matter exists and that everything can be understood and expressed by mathematics. Information is a problem for naturalists. Everyone believes in information and its control over matter, particularly genetic material. Although information controls matter there is no evidence that matter produces information. The religious or faith hypothesis about this fact is that matter does produce information and we have not discovered how yet. The more scientific hypothesis is that information is supernatural. In the beginning was information or relationships which come from a trinitarian and relational God. Matter is created, not self-begotten.

Thursday

A time, times and half a time

In Revelation 12:14 we read that the Church flees to the desert, where she is taken care of for a time, times and half a time. This adds up to three and a half, which is half of seven. Seven means perfect or complete in Biblical symbolism. John wrote Revelation not long after the crucifixion of Jesus. Can this mean that half of human history happened before Jesus and half will happen after? Did Jesus come to die for everyone right in the middle of human history? Jesus is the center of everything.

Friday

News and Propaganda

We need news to inform us and propaganda to motivate us. News is neutral facts. Propaganda is advocacy. News and Propaganda are usually combined. If all news becomes advocacy or propaganda the people have less and less in common. Propaganda can be honest or dishonest. Evangelism should be honest propaganda advocating a worldview and promoting the Kingdom of God. If we pay for news that is mostly propaganda, we get what we pay for and distort truth and culture. Stay awake and test everything.

Week Eight

Monday

Our Crown of Glory

Christians look forward to receiving a crown of reward and glory from God. In I Thessalonians 2:19-20 Paul shows us that our crown, glory and joy is other people. The growth of life and beauty in other people that results from our serving them will be our joy forever in the presence of Jesus. If I am your eternal crown, you will want to take very good care of me – to protect me, polish me and perhaps bang the dents out of me. You are my reward and I am your reward. God help us to remember that. Amen.

Tuesday

Peace

Peace or Shalom is not a lack of conflict. It is the foundation and framework of reality given by God for meaning and stability in conflict. If people see conflict in the context of eternity and God's Truth, they will have a more realistic perspective, avoiding prejudice and selfishness. Peace must function in reality rather than in romantic fantasy. If Christians truly act as salt and light in the world, peace will increase. Pray for the Peace of God (Je ru salem).

Wednesday

Pentecost II

The Holy Spirit is the Spirit of Christ Who enters us and bears fruit – love, joy, peace, patience, kindness, goodness, faithfulness, gentleness, and self-control. Christians have different and special gifts. Normally all Christians increase in all the fruits. By these fruits we can measure our growth as God's children and be comforted about our salvation. The Holy Spirit teaches us to pray and ask for what God wants us to have. Pray to the Father in the Name of the Son, through the power of the Holy Spirit. Amen.

Thursday

Postmodern 10 Commandments

(On two Samsung tablets)

I. Thou shalt value only that which contributes to the flourishing of thy life as thou seeist it.

II. Thou shalt not honor or serve any person, institution, or values other than thyself.

III. Thou shalt not submit to any linguistic conventions that are in any way offensive to thyself at any moment.

IV. Thou shalt order the schedule and rhythm of thy life only according to thy feelings about it.

V. Thou shalt honor thyself and thy convenience above all other people.

continued on page 256

Friday

One, Two or Three?

If "all is One" all relationships are evil and unreal. If all is two there is no subjectivity, only duality. It was not good for Adam to be alone because "God alone is God and God is not alone". Only the God of the Bible is a reasonable basis and explanation for the reality we experience. God is Love because He is Three and loves among Himself. There is goodness in our evil and crumbling world because of God. Trust in Him, Father, Son and Holy Spirit. Worship and obey Him alone. Accept no counterfeit substitutes.

Week Nine

Monday

Pray in Jesus' Name

Jesus promised anything we ask God in His Name will be given to us. "Name" isn't a label or a magic word. It means the nature and character and will of Jesus. If we ask for whatever we imagine would be good and add Jesus' name to the prayer the promise is not valid. Praying in His Name means praying for what He wants for us. Why would God give us something He doesn't want us to have? It would not bless us. The goal of praying is to relate to God and be more like Jesus.

Tuesday

Choose Life!

Life is hard and complicated; death is easy and simple. Choose life! We can choose death but we don't have to; it will happen to us naturally. But we do have to choose life. Life is hard, death is easy. Our natural life just happens "naturally" but our spiritual life (complete life) must be received from God, chosen and lived. Life is possible because of the death and resurrection of Jesus Christ. We cannot make life. Only God makes life. We only need to receive it from Him. Make life a habit. Be thankful. God bless you.

Wednesday

Prayer I

Prayer is special and ordinary. It is special and wonderful to be able to speak to the Creator of the Universe and know that He hears us and cares about us and what we say to Him. Prayer is ordinary because we can pray at any moment of the day or night for two seconds or two minutes. We can pray in the middle of working or a conversation or reading or driving (maybe don't close your eyes). Prayer is ordinary because it brings order into our lives in both time and eternity. Prayer is essential for life.

Thursday

Prophets, Priests and Kings

Not many Christians think of themselves as prophets, priests or kings. A prophet tells God's Truth; past, present or future. A priest is a bridge builder making a connection between people and God by prayer. A king gives order and guidelines and makes judgements about what is around. We know that Jesus is Prophet, Priest and King. When we believe in Jesus and belong to Him we take on those roles in the world around us; in our families, our friendships, our workplace, our Churches and communities. This is God's calling for Christians in the world.

Friday

Reading the Bible

Reading the Bible every day is important because it keeps us in focus with God's Kingdom and Reality. It is a window into God's stable Truth that works as an anchor for us during days that might otherwise be confusing and out of focus. It also keeps us connected with others who read the same passages, even at a distance. The benefit of reading doesn't depend on our perfectly understanding everything we read. May God give us an appetite for His Word. Amen.

Week Ten

Monday

Reality I

Reality is who God is, what He does and what He wants. God is original and infinitely powerful to sustain this reality and make us healthy and happy in it. If we try to live in a reality made by people, past or present, we imitate the serpent/devil, who rebelled and tried to make his own reality, which results in death. We are attracted to a false reality because we believe the myth that in it we will be autonomous and authentic. May God help us to learn about reality from His Word and give us the wisdom and power to choose life. Amen.

Tuesday

Culture

Culture is cultivating or growing things together and developing what we value. We have cultures of family, sport, business, nation. There are cultures of life and death, hope and despair, the Kingdom of God and of this world, love and selfishness. Christians are called to be aware of the culture around them and to contribute to it. Salt and light give flavor and clarity to the world. Being salt and light is blessing the city with the values of the Kingdom of God. Worshiping culture leads to a culture of death. Worshiping God leads to a culture of life.

Wednesday

Christian Patriotism

How can we Christians love our countries? We can pray for the leaders, even if they persecute us. Treasure and fight for our marriages. Commit random acts of kindness. Take control by going the second mile. Bless our neighbors by word and action in the Name of Jesus. Light even a small candle rather than make loud curses against the darkness. Build exemplary reputations for hard work, helpfulness, and dependability. Pray and look for ways to be part of the solution rather than part of the problem. Depend on God, ourselves and each other rather than government aid.

Thursday

Salt and Light

The world is the salt and light of the Church. Jesus said the opposite in the Sermon on the Mount. Jesus wants the Church to be the clarity and flavor of the world. It is often the other way around. The values of the world – success, relevance, market share, political correctness and social acceptance often get more attention than the values of the Kingdom of God – the fruits of the Spirit and faithfulness to His Word. Christians should be original and different in making culture, not just follow the world around to copy it.

Friday

Security

God is Love. God is three Persons. God created everything that is. The foundation of the universe is not matter and energy but love. God loves you. If you receive God's love and remain in it, you are kept and held in the arms of the creator of the universe. You are secure. All other "securities" are temporary and incomplete. In a fallen world many negative things happen to us – accident, sickness, persecution, unemployment, alienation and finally death. None of these things can make us fundamentally insecure when we belong to God. Receive God's Love and trust in it!

Week Eleven

Monday

Sin

God is the original uncreated reality. Everything created expressed Who He is in its original form. Trying to change reality according to our own imagination is sin. Sin is trying to be God. God is other centered. The devil became selfcentered, which is sin. Moses taught "Do not steal.". Jesus taught "Do not want to steal.". Sin is more an attitude than an act. God is love. Sin is what does not conform to God's Character and Word and is not motivated by love. Life is not possible in alternate realities, so the product of sin is death.

Tuesday

Singleness

God's plan or default program for humans includes marriage, children, productive and creative work, and a healthy body and mind. None of us fits this template perfectly. God calls us in our limitations but not to them. We all have special needs. Our needs are finally fully met only in Jesus. We also need to be aware of each other's brokenness and pray and do something to make it as much better as possible. We don't know the extent of each other's lack of fulfillment, but we should do what we can to help.

Wednesday

Heaven on Earth

Jesus taught us to pray "Your Kingdom come, Your Will be done, on Earth as it is in Heaven." Jesus wants the supernatural dimensions of Heaven to come to us here, not for us to go "there". Our true and eternal citizenship is in Heaven, but we won't go there to get it. It will come here when Jesus appears again. Christianity is not a life through escape but through engagement. Suffering and confusion have made Christians think of God taking us someplace else, rather than coming to be with us here. Let's come into focus with God's plan.

Thursday

Speaking of God

In Isaiah 62:6 we read "You who make mention of the Lord, do not keep silent." Do you mention the Lord by saying "God bless you" to your neighbors, colleagues, grocery clerks, doctors and bankers? Sometimes people have been startled when I did that, but they did not seem offended. People need God's blessing. Try bringing God into your conversations in appropriate, positive and inviting ways. We should be excited rather than embarrassed or shy about the Lord. When you bless people pray for them. God give us grace, courage and wisdom to speak of Him. Amen.

Friday

Controversial

Many Christians and others fear saying or doing anything controversial and warn against it. If something is not controversial it is universally accepted. Very little is uni-versally accepted. Perhaps we agree about gravity and day following night, but not the flatness or the age of the earth. Nothing is more controversial than the Gospel of Jesus Christ. Christians should be peace makers but should not pretend there is peace when there isn't. Controversy cannot be avoided and will be with us until Jesus appears. Faith is trusting God when our situation is not safe, not pretending it is safe.

Week Twelve

Monday

Take up your Cross

Jesus said, "Whoever wants to be my disciple must deny themselves and take up their cross daily and follow me." Jesus took up His Cross, which was the burden of the sins of others. Our cross is not something that happens to us, it is something we actively take up to carry the burden of others. We are not victims of our cross, we are change agents because we take up our cross. Our cross is not sickness or job loss or earthquake. God presents our cross to us in the people and situations we meet. Take it up.

Tuesday

Taste

"De Gustibus Non Est Disputandum" – Taste is not debatable. Our taste is part of who we are, but it is not safe. If we think something is good because we like it or bad because we don't like it, we worship ourselves and lack truth. Liking something tells us about ourselves, not about the thing itself. Taste is subjective and must be married to objectivity to bring forth life. Two confessions will bring freedom: I like what is unworthy and I don't like what is worthy. Don't trust your taste to teach you truth. If we didn't like sin we would never do it.

Wednesday

The Blood of Jesus

In a sinful world covered by the dust of death, we live by the death of others. God has given us animals who have died to give us food, clothing and shelter all through history. The blood of these animals points to the Blood of Jesus, which glues our broken selves and broken world together. Jesus loves us so much He gave His Blood for us so we can have new life and be with Him and each other in God's Kingdom forever. Our lives are precious and beautiful to God. We should take care of ourselves by caring for and serving others.

Thursday

The Default Program

God's default program for human life involves marriage and children, good health, productivity, and trust in Him. None of us fit the program fully so there are special programs like singleness, growth through adversity and contentment in limitations. All of us are handicapped. Some of the handicaps are obvious and some are hidden. Some handicaps can be healed during our lifetime and some not. We should be sensitive and sympathetic to our handicaps and those of others. Be realistic and look for God's victory in your handicapped condition. Encourage and support others in their special situations.

Friday

The Kingdom of God

Jesus said the Kingdom is near, coming, here, among us and inside us. This does not describe the Church or someplace far away. The Kingdom of God is the rule of God in the world, in our societies and families and in our hearts. "Your Kingdom come" and "Your Will be done" mean the same thing. Jesus wants the rule of God to come on the earth. We should want it with Him. God, help us to want your will and receive it first in our hearts and then reaching out to others. Amen.

Week Thirteen

Monday

Gifts and Fruits

From the Holy Spirit we have gifts and fruits. The fruits are normative while the gifts are not. Different Christians have different gifts. If you are missing some of the gifts; if you have never spoken in tongues or raised anyone from the dead, your life can still be a normal Christian life. If you are missing any of the fruits (Love, Joy, Peace, Patience, Kindness, Goodness, Faithfulness, Gentleness and Self-control) your life is sub-normal. All the fruits are for each and every Christian. The fruits are a better way of taking your spiritual temperature than the gifts. May God help us to strengthen the fruits that are weak. Amen.

Tuesday

Attachment and Freedom

There once was a man who knew from faith and experience all his life that desire and attachment bring suffering. His hope was that after many lifetimes he might attain liberation by realizing absolute oneness. Then the uncreated creator, one and many, met him and promised to give him a new self. The uncreated creator emptied himself into the man and he became a new and other centered self. Then he awakened and realized he could have desire for Truth and attachment to loved ones without suffering for eternity. His liberation was a gift, not an attainment.

Wednesday

What We Deserve

A lot of discussion goes on about what people deserve or don't deserve. If something unpleasant happens we tend to say, "I don't deserve that.". The wages of sin is death. We all sin so we all deserve to die. God gives us the "right" to receive forgiveness and life through Jesus Christ, not because we deserve it but because God is Love and wants to graciously give them to us. If we truly deserve anything there is no Grace, which means giving good that is not deserved. To get what we deserve is a terrifying possibility.

Thursday

Judgement

Judgement is for correction or destruction. To judge is to make right or fitting and belonging. We don't fit with God because our sins have misshapen us. God's judgment restores our proper shape. The process can be painful and frightening, and we accept it by faith, trusting in God. Those who accept God's salvation through Jesus Christ are blessed by His judgment and made whole and perfect. Those who reject God's salvation are destroyed by His judgment. The refining fire purifies or burns up. Lord, help us to receive your loving judgment and healing. Amen.

Friday

Communion

Communion is a family meal that believers in Jesus share for remembering the incar-nation and sacrifice of Jesus and for fellow-ship. Eating and drinking are ordinary things and basic to human life. Jesus didn't give us natural things like spring water and wild berries but artistic things – bread and wine. We add our creative work of dominion to what God has created and bring what we make to the meal. The meal is only for those who recognize the power of the body and blood of Jesus and their own need of them for forgiveness, healing and new life.

Week Fourteen

Monday

God's Law of Love

God's Law in the Sermon on the Mount is about loving relationships with each other. It is not about nationality, geography, diet, ceremonies, race, culture, or heritage. These things are valid parts of our Christian lives, but if they interfere with loving each other they become idolatry. We should not eliminate or ignore these things, but we should make sure they support and encourage loving each other. All the values and activities of our lives should serve love. Love belongs at the top of the hierarchy and gives meaning and life to everything else. Think love.

Tuesday

Luck

Many people don't believe in God. I some-times say "God bless you" to them anyway because I believe in God and that He can bless them. Many people say "Good luck" to me although I don't believe in luck or chance. Chance always works out 50-50 so nothing happens by chance. People think of luck as the forces of an impersonal mechanical universe moving their lives around or as personalized "lady luck". The hope or wish for good luck is hopeless and random. We live in a personal reality where God sees and cares about everything. God bless you.

Wednesday

The Parable of the Banana Peel

If I get up late and am running on the platform to catch a train to the airport to go on a mission, I might slip on a banana peel and break my ankle. How am I to understand the situation? Is it caused by my sin of getting up late? Is it caused by the sin of the banana eater? Is it caused by the devil to prevent people being blessed on the mission? Is it caused by God because the train is going to crash down the track? All things work for good for those who love the Lord. My job is not to figure everything out but to love the Lord and my neighbors.

Thursday

Special and Ordinary

Each of us has special or unique experiences and events in our lives as well as ordinary ones. Special experiences like dreams, visions, healings, large group meetings are encouraging and memorable, usually not repeatable. Ordinary things like discipline, prayer habits, covering people's sins with our love, the basic grid of our worldview give order and structure or a frame to our lives and world. The special and the ordinary are both essential and need to be in focus and coordination with each other. Together they make a whole and clear view of the world and our lives.

Friday

The Unforgivable Sin

Some Christians worry they might have committed the unforgivable sin, blasphemy against the Holy Spirit, and be permanently separated from God. Sin is acting and speaking but is more deeply an attitude. Blasphemy against the Holy Spirit is the attitude that His work is evil, particularly His testimony about Jesus Christ. People who have this attitude cannot repent and be forgiven because they believe they are right. People who worry about this sin have most probably not done it or they wouldn't care. People who have committed it are satisfied with themselves.

Week Fifteen

Monday

Pentecost I

Pentecost is the 50th. day after Easter when the Holy Spirit came with new and special power on believers in Jesus to speak to others about God and be understood in every language. God is Love. The power of the Holy Spirit enables us to live in loving relationships and community. The gifts of the Holy Spirit are for serving others. Spirit is wind. The Holy Spirit blows on us and in us to proclaim Jesus and gives us gifts to help us bless others, particularly through teaching them about Jesus, and God's loving salvation. He teaches us how we need to change and be healed.

Tuesday

Truth and Meaning

Truth does not equal fact. Truth equals fact plus meaning. Meaning means relationships, which means that nothing and no one has meaning in itself. Anything that is only self-referential has no meaning. The meaning of the color red is not in the color red but in its relationships with blue, green, brown, etc. The meaning of Adam at the creation was pointedly not in Adam (it is not good for man to be alone) but in his relationships with God and Eve. The meaning of Jesus is not in Jesus but in His relationships with the Father and the Holy Spirit. Truth is relational.

Wednesday

Hallowed Be Thy Name

Someone's name is not only a label. It is also the character or reputation. "Hallowed be Thy Name" is not a complement or statement. It is a request that God's Name will be hallowed, or known as holy, on the earth. This is the first request in the Lord's Prayer because it is our greatest need. God's Name is often known as "myth" or "optional" or "fantasy". This mistake inhibits people from coming to Him. The main task of God's people from Abraham to the present is to live and speak so His Name is known as Holy.

Thursday

Need

Independence is a basic value of our time. We are taught that we can invent ourselves and be anything we want to be. It is a widespread principle that we should not marry someone if we need them. We should be independent and self-sufficient. This results in people not valuing each other and coming to despise each other after the fun wears off. God made people to need each other, especially in marriage. Christians should identify clear areas of need and thank God when He supplies that need through the person they marry. May God help us to serve and depend on each other. Amen.

Friday

Veganism

The main point of veganism is against the commodification of animals: People should not own, exploit, buy or sell animals. Living like this is only possible with the support of modern technology for transportation, agriculture and synthetic fabrics for clothing. The vegan diet is part of the picture. Veganism excludes the owning of animal pets. The big question is whether humans are responsible for organizing the other animals, as the Bible teaches, or humans should live like vegetarian animals without using animals to support civilization. To decide this it is important to know whether nature is perfect or broken.

Week Sixteen

Monday

What is Love?

Love is not an emotion, attachment or appetite. Love is not centered on the self but on the other. The center of Jesus is not Jesus but the Father and the Holy Spirit. The center of the Father and the Holy Spirit is the other two Persons of God. Each Person of God empties Himself into the other two to supply and sustain them. This means that each Person is emptied once and filled twice so there is a constant increase. Love is a series of responsible choices and actions by which we encourage and enable the loved one to be who God made them to be.

Tuesday

Worship

Worship is "worth ship" or telling someone how much value they have. We worship God or money or advertisers or cultural norms by praising them in word and song, investing in them, imitating them and obeying them. Worship is 24/7. It doesn't stop when the meeting ends. We come to Church for "worship prep", to be prepared to worship on Monday and every day. Our worship of many things is forced and exaggerated. Worship of God is free and can never be exaggerated. We can praise Him wholeheartedly knowing He will never be unworthy of our praise and worship.

Wednesday

200% Reality

Naturalistic science has taught us to understand reality in terms of 100%. But if we put things like God's Sovereignty and people's free will on a two dimensional pie chart it never divides up well. We end up with no sovereignty or no free will. The Bible adds a 100% supernatural reality. If we use a three-dimensional sphere chart, we can see a 100% plane of Sovereignty and a 100% plane of free will. Sovereignty and free don't compete for space, they omplement each other in a marriage relationship. Christians are not equal to God. They are 100% committed.

Thursday

Chance

God built the function of cause and effect into the creation. We cannot completely observe or understand cause and effect. In human observation many things happen by chance in that they are unpredictable. Chance is not a motivator or cause of events. Events take place through chance and through time but not by chance or time. If we flip a coin 10 times, we might perceive a tendency towards heads or tails. Over time and con-tinuing coin flips the tendency disappears. Nothing happens by chance. Things happen by the Will of God and the will of His personal creatures.

Friday

Death

Death is basically alienation or separation. People are bundles of life with mind, will, emotions, and body all held together by a glue called the soul. If you lose your soul, you lose the glue and fall apart. What makes the glue sticky is the blood of Jesus that cleans the person and keeps them together in life. Physical death is a separation of the parts but people who have the blood of Jesus get put together again forever at the resurrection. We also experience death of relationships, trust, hope, and ideas. Look to Jesus for victory over death.

Week Seventeen

Monday

Abundant Life

If you would ask 10 people at random whether their life would get larger or smaller if they became a Christian what do you think they would say? Some Christians think they can keep their lives pure by avoiding most literature, music and cinema. The Apostle Paul did that when he was legalistic. When he became a Christian, he was free to read and memorize the Greek pagan poets and even quoted a hymn to Zeus in his sermon in Athens (Acts 17). May God help us to love our neighbors by learning about what is in their minds and hearts. Amen.

Tuesday

A Parable of Hurt and Healing

Once there was a little girl who was hurt, rejected and bullied in various ways. She built a wall around herself and effectively shut out the pain. Her highest priority was to avoid pain. Loneliness, anxieties, fears and other problems developed. She was unhappy and unwell. Then she realized she had been trying to be her own God and protector and had crippled herself. She turned to God in confession and was forgiven. She turned to God in trust for protection and true identity in Jesus Christ and the healing process began.

Wednesday

Be at Peace or Don't Care?

We are forbidden to worry or be anxious about anything and promised God's Peace about everything. Sometimes being at peace leads to not caring anymore or disengaging. How can we be at peace about our job or health or a struggle in our family or Church and remain engaged and effective? This is a special energy from the Holy Spirit, a passive activity, a restful urgency, a dynamic passivism, faith and works married in the Christian life. Ask for this experience and look for it. Resting in the Lord gives us energy to serve.

Thursday

Blessing and Cursing

Bless means to make life larger, fuller, richer. Curse means to make life smaller. They can be statements or rituals but are much more. Blessing can be money, health, knowledge, encouragement, help, rebukes, and challenges to be better. Blessings make us real. Curses make us unreal. Blessings are often painful while curses are often pleasurable. The dentist is an example of a painful blessing. Flattery is an example of an enjoyable curse. Blessings move us to engage with life and growth. Curses distract us from life and encourage us to shrink.

Friday

Calling

There are ordinary, general callings, which Christians have in common and specific callings to each of us. The ordinary callings, giving order to our lives, is to believe in Jesus, become God's child, love each other and bear the fruits of the Spirit. Special callings are being married, studying medicine or plumbing, holding an office in the Church, being a faithful employee, going on missions, starting an NGO. If concentrating on a special calling interferes with loving each other, we lose touch with the ordinary calling and our lives go out of order. Keeping first things first brings blessing.

Week Eighteen

Monday

Christianity is Ordinary

Coming to believe in Jesus Christ and being born again was the most special thing that had ever happened in his life. He was very excited and tried to repeat the thrilling experience and emotion. This took a lot of effort and sometimes he had to pretend to himself and others. Gradually he realized the special things didn't give the order and stability he needed. The Ordinary, faithful values and habits of Christianity became the dependable foundation for his life. Special experiences are proper for special occasions. The Ordinary things give constant, faithful goodness to our lives.

Tuesday

Examining Ourselves

In 1 Cor. 11 Paul teaches us to examine ourselves and not take communion in an unworthy manner, but recognize the body and blood of the Lord. This does not mean to confess our sins and become pure and worthy. It means to know that we are unworthy and recognize the body and blood of Jesus as the only way to become worthy. When we know that we are saved by Jesus, then we can joyfully take the bread and the wine with each other. We become worthy when we know we are unworthy. Trust in Jesus alone.

Wednesday

Draw Near to God

At the end of a dramatic personal testimony in Psalm 73, Asaph wrote "But as for me, it is good to draw near to God." God is always reaching from Heaven to be near us. We can draw near to Him by remembering Him and lifting ourselves up to Him, remembering He is always giving us life, protecting us, keeping us, enabling us. In the stress and struggles of life we can be stabilized and have a realistic perspective by remembering Him and His powerful Love for us. Be with Him day and night.

Thursday

Entertainment and Education

Entertainment holds people between one active part of life and another in a suspended animation of enjoyment. Education is drawing people out and forward into fuller awareness, engagement, and learning. Entertainment can make education more pleasant but cannot replace it. Entertainment can be a blessing or enlargement for life. Education always is. Entertainment leaves people where they were. Education leads them forward. Entertainment gives the people what they want. Education gives the people what they need. Entertainment is cool. Education is hot. Entertainers can be popular and rich. Educators, believing in Jesus, bless and are blessed forever.

Friday

Equality

In many ways people are not equal: in health, intelligence, education, earning power, family background and inheritance. We are all equal in our need for God's Grace and salvation. Righteousness is like a balloon full of air. If you smash it with a big hammer it becomes a limp rag of rubber. If you just prick it with a tiny pin the same thing happens. In my need for God's forgiveness I am equal to a murdering mafia drug dealer. Some sins cause more damage than others but all of them bring death. We can't look down on anyone.

Week Nineteen

Monday

Self-control and Spirit control

The Bible teaches us to "Get a new heart and a right spirit" and "never be lacking in zeal but keep your spiritual fervor". This is impossible to do on our own. God promises to "give us a new heart and put a right spirit in us" and tells us to walk with Spirit and keep in step with the Spirit. We are most truly in control of ourselves when the Spirit controls us. The Christian life is 100% active and 100% passive. Be Israel – the one who wrestles with (not against) God for Truth and life.

Tuesday

Rights and Responsibilities

The Bible is aware of the needs of people. It cares for those needs by giving people responsibilities for each other. The Bible doesn't seem to know anything about "rights". Responsibilities are other centered. Rights are self-centered. The world's main moral imperative is to find out what life owes us and devote ourselves to collecting. In the Kingdom of God, we find out our responsibilities and how we can contribute to make life work. We owe life, life doesn't owe us. Rights cancel Grace. Responsibilities receive Grace. When we lose our life in Christ, we find it.

Wednesday

Spiritual = Supernatural

Most people believe this equation, that spiritual means invisible, non-physical. The Bible teaches us it is false. The birth and resurrection of Jesus were spiritual and pointedly physical. If the physical birth and resurrection are not spiritual, we have lost Christmas and Easter. Our spiritual lives are physical, intellectual, emotional, relational and supernatural. The spiritual kingdom of God includes a physical, new earth. Jesus died to make us whole and complete. Anything that makes us incomplete or divided is unspiritual. God does not want us to be split into spiritual and non-spiritual parts, but to be whole. Spiritual = Totally Real.

Thursday

Full Time Christians

Many Christians speak of going into "full time Christian work.". More recently people say, "go into Ministry.". Christians should always be full time Christians and in ministry or service in various ways. All of us are prophets, priests and kings. Whether our funding comes from tithe money or from the local economy does not make a big difference. There is no class system in Christianity and no part time Christian. We should all take responsibility for service and full time Christian life. Be a full time Christian plumber or pastor. Be all you can be for Jesus.

Friday

Fasting

The Bible assumes fasting as part of the Christian life. We can fast from food, conversation, reading, screen time, internet and other things. Fasting is usually for special purposes like repentance, thanksgiving, deciding on a job or a spouse, joining a Church, preparing for College. It can be for ourselves and/or for others. Fasting makes us weak and helps us know our need for God. Fasting sharpens the mind and helps us pray and receive God's guidance. Fasting is not magic and should not be a spiritual Olympics contest. It should not be overdone and damage our health.

Week Twenty

Monday

Follow Your Heart

This is very popular advice. It expresses the humanistic belief that there is good inside everyone that can infallibly, authentically guide us in our lives if we look inside ourselves and find it. If the Bible is true, our hearts are deceptive and undependable and should not be trusted. We should trust in God's Word and test every impulse of our hearts by it. It is attractive to believe that what feels right is right. My feelings express "my truth", which isolates me from every-one else's truth. Your heart will tell you many things. Test them all.

Tuesday

Shame

Shame, or a sense of worthlessness is painful. If that pain drives us to Jesus, we can have new and eternal worth from Him and despise the shame. If shame doesn't bring us to Jesus, it produces bitterness, resentfulness and hatred. It damages and distorts us. If we shame others to make ourselves look and feel better or to dominate them, we should be ashamed. Shame is poverty of spirit, which we need to have God's Kingdom. Don't fear shame or deal with it by yourself. Bring it to Jesus. He loves you and will do something about it.

Wednesday

Freedom to Fail

All Christians are sinners and broken. God intends us to be perfect and we are not, which is frustrating. When non-Christians fail their self-made identities can be shattered. When Christians fail, they can be forgiven and lifted up by Jesus. We don't want to fail at anything, but Jesus gives us freedom to fail without panic and move forward in hope and trust. When you fail, don't wallow in shame. Bring the failure to God openly in prayer. See the failure in the perspective of God's eternal Grace and Love. Receive His Peace, comfort and power for life.

Thursday

Give Thanks in All Circumstances

Christians live in many different circumstances: health and sickness, wealth and poverty, safety and danger, popularity and isolation. The universal and eternal Truth of God's saving and living Gospel in Jesus Christ is what Christians have in common. This Truth works out in each different situation. Our circumstances, whether pleasant or unpleasant, can make us forget God's Love and be unthankful. God's Love surrounds all our circumstances. We should not be thankful for all circumstances because some are evil. If we remember God's Love, we can be realistically thankful, which is healthy and encouraging for us.

Friday

Language I

God speaks and is faithful to what He says. People made in His image are intended to speak and be faithful to what they say. When we lose our respect for language and our commitment to the meaning of words, we depend more on facial expressions, body language, emotional energy, social associations and our own appetites for communication. This process feels good and is attractive because it is more relaxed than diligence and commitment. While nonverbal elements of communication are valid, this process also makes us more like animals and less like God. Be careful. Choose life.

Week Twenty One

Monday

The Elephant in the Room

An elephant is a popular illustration for a defense of relativism. The elephant represents truth, while blind people are trying to find out what truth is. The people find the trunk, tail, leg and side of the elephant and say truth is a hose, rope, tree or wall. The point is we need to accept and tolerate each other's truth journeys to have total truth. The problem is that the elephant is silent and passive and doesn't help us know him. God is an active, personal Truth who tells us about Himself and everything else.

Tuesday

God's Promises

Many of God's promises are already fulfilled, either for people of long ago or for the whole community. They cannot be claimed by individuals. One promise that can be claimed by each of us is in Philippians 4:6-7. God promises that if we bring everything to Him, He will keep us in Christ Jesus. Our deepest need is to be wanted, kept and to belong. This is the promise we really need. This is the promise God always keeps for each of us. When we claim this promise our whole lives are cradled and sustained by God's Love.

Wednesday

Authority

Authority is the power to describe reality as an author describes a book. All authority comes from God, the author of reality. As children need parents to describe the reality of bedtime, diet and where to play safely, we need God to describe reality to us. He does this in the Bible and by the Holy Spirit. Authority functions in the relationships of God/people, parents/children, government/citizens, husbands/wives, employers/employees, elders/members of Churches and others. All the relationships are distorted by sin. Freedom comes from working and praying to correct the relationships, not eliminating authority. Pray for those who have authority.

Thursday

Grace

He made damaging mistakes at work. His boss forgave him because he had hired him and trained him and hoped for him for the future. This is Grace, given by the powerful to the needy. By the power of the Holy Spirit we can give Grace to others. Weak, simple and despised Christians have the power from God to give grace to anyone. If Christians look at everyone through the lens of Grace, they become salt and light in the world and instruments of God's Peace. The weak hide behind their rights or supposed superiority. The strong give Grace.

Friday

The Battle

If we teach our children that gender is a gift and not something we choose for ourselves according to our feelings; that we do not invent ourselves and Jesus only is Lord, it will bring our children and us into strong conflict at school and in our culture in general. Our situation as Christians is not safe, but God is with us. The culture around us teaches us and our children deadly, unbiblical ideas and demands that we conform to them. Where should we draw a line and take a stand? May God give us wisdom and courage. Amen.

Week Twenty Two

Monday

Total Freedom = Death

In our culture freedom is increasingly valued over form, loyalty, responsibility, dependability, or obedience. People were not made by God to be alone or independent. If we become totally free from our need for each other as individuals or society, we move toward alienation and isolation, which is death. People want to be free in terms of their imagination, but our imagination doesn't produce reality. Reality is Who God is, what He does and what He wants. Freedom is lively and has meaning only with form. God, help us to be free in the forms You give us. Amen.

Tuesday

Hospitality

Welcoming strangers (Hospes) or enemies (Hostis) is a normal part of the Christian life. Christian hospitality is welcoming those who need a welcome and cannot pay us back. Giving parties for friends doesn't count. People can be welcomed into our houses, our time, our friendship. Hospitality is for fellow believers especially but also for unbelievers. Hospitality might be limited by special family needs for privacy. National hospitality in the Old Testament included conforming to Jewish religion and culture. We prepare a culture for visitors in our houses or communities. Visitors are not invited to shape our culture. Cultivate Xenophilia.

Wednesday

Offensive

Being "offensive" is an accusation against which there is no defense. If a person feels offended or annoyed or attacked, the feeling is not debatable. To offend is to attack, rather than to defend. If you say something others do not agree with, you attack their beliefs. If you only agree and never offend there can be no discussion or debate. We will be reduced to silence and being controlled by the loudest voice or the biggest stick. The Gospel of Jesus Christ is offensive because it denies the belief that a person is fine and doesn't need God.

Thursday

Personal

By personal most people mean the self. Biblically it includes the other. God is a Personal God. He is not a Person but three Persons. He is Personal because of His relationships before the beginning of time. The image of God is "them". Everything else in the creation was good but it was not good for Adam to be alone because God is not alone. Jesus is a Personal Savior because He is personal and He saves, not because I personally believe in Him. Personal doesn't begin with me. It begins with God Who is Love. Trust in Him.

Friday

The Cloud of Glory

The Cloud of God's Glory or Presence is found throughout Scripture and is an interface between the natural and supernatural dimensions. The Cloud helps us understand many events like the burning bush, the Exodus, smoking Mt. Sinai, the tabernacle and temple presence of God, the star of Bethlehem, the Transfiguration, the Ascension, Paul's conversion and the second appearing of Jesus. The Cloud is experienced as fire, light, darkness, or star and is never water vapor. The experience of the Cloud seems to happen while awake and often includes a voice. May God help us to see more of the whole picture. Amen.

Week Twenty Three

Monday

Knowing Jesus

Knowing Jesus includes right teaching and information about Him and experience of or with Him through obedience and imitation. Some people get a lot of information about Jesus but don't experience much healing or change. Some people have a lot of experiences with Jesus but don't really know much about Him. It is easy to figure out which side we lean on. A healthy Christian life involves gently leaning on the more neglected side. God bless us and guide us and make our lives more complete. Amen.

Tuesday

Meditation

Meditation is nonlinear cognitive activity. It works in a sphere or force field. Non-Christian meditation centers on the self and doesn't go anywhere. Biblical meditation is more passive than thought or prayer. It is being open to insights about God and life from the Holy Spirit and the Bible. It focuses on parts of God's character like His unfailing love or infinite power, which are mysterious and cannot be understood completely by the rational mind. Other forms of meditation can be therapeutic in limited ways. Christian meditation is connected to prayer and part of a full life in Christ.

Wednesday

Stereo Vision

Having the mind of Christ includes having a single stereo vision of reality. We can look at events and circumstances we are experiencing as with a microscope. We can also look at the eternal promises of God as with a telescope. Christian vision uses the microscope and telescope at the same time, giving us a true stereo vision. Bring your life into focus with God's eternity and apply God's eternal promises to your life at the same time. Don't switch back and forth. The Holy Spirit gives us clear depth of vision. Ask for it and use it.

Thursday

Pray Constantly

How do we pray constantly? If we talk to God all the time, we can never talk to anyone else. Perhaps this situation is like at school or work. We don't talk to the teacher or the boss all the time, but they are in the room and everything we do is somehow related to them. They are a reference and guide for us. God is always in the room and He is the Boss. All of our thinking, acting and interacting can be in reference to God and have a solid and eternal meaning.

Friday

Prayer II

Prayer is not meditation, contemplation, thinking, imagining, feeling, action or work, communion with nature, ecstatic or transcendental experience, Union with the "ALL", silence ritual or magic. Prayer is not natural but is given by God as part of our full spiritual life with Him. Prayer is personal communication between one person and another Person. Prayer is language – direct, definite, and committed. In the Bible God's people speak to Him in ordinary language. God speaks to us through His Word and creation. We can respond by speaking to Him about His Word that brings us life. Return to God. Bring words with you.

Week Twenty Four

Monday

Beauty

The dictionary tells us that beauty is attractiveness, mostly to the eyes but also in usefulness or convenience. This kind of beauty is completely subjective to the individual or culture. The Bible contextualizes beauty with holiness or what is attractive to God: humility, faithfulness, obedience, service. Jesus was not physically attractive on earth and is completely and eternally beautiful. Beauty that is not attractive to God will end. Beauty that belongs in God's Kingdom is eternal. We can make and do things that are beautiful in both ways. Always see every-thing in the context of eternal beauty and life.

Tuesday

Visible and Invisible

"As the body without the spirit is dead, so faith without deeds is dead." James 2:26. The physical, visible body is dead without the invisible spirit. The invisible faith is dead without the visible deeds. The visible and invisible belong together and work together for life. You cannot be spiritual without a physical body. Your physical body cannot live without the spirit. The devil wants us to choose one or the other. Jesus wants us to have both. Choose a full life in Christ. Keep the visible and invisible parts of your life coordinated, with God's help.

Wednesday

Guidance

God's Will is perfect, and He wants us to make responsible choices. Christians make two kinds of mistakes when making decisions: 1. Making them all on our own without any reference to God. 2. Expecting God to tell us exactly what to do so we can blame Him if anything goes wrong. If we say "God told me" no one can discuss our decision with us without arguing with God. There are no perfect choices, only responsible ones. God guides us through Scripture, visions, dreams, finances, words of other people, circumstances and more. We are also free and responsible.

Thursday

Meaning of Meaning

Meaning means relationships. That means that nothing has meaning in itself. The meaning of the color red is not in the color red, but in its relationships with green, blue, yellow, etc. The meaning of Adam in the creation account was pointedly not in him-self (it is not good for the man to be alone). The meaning of Adam is in his relationships with God (which is not enough) and also with Eve. The meaning of Jesus is not in Jesus but in His relationships with the Father and the Holy Spirit. Meaning is a function of love.

Friday

How We Know

Knowing what words mean and sharing those meanings is essential but not adequate for knowing truth. Knowing friends is more than knowing their name and its meaning. We know rationally, experientially, emotionally, socially and by revelation. If we expect too much of language, we will get frustrated. If we are not committed to what we say we will get sloppy and unstable. Language must be faithfully treasured and used in context with other ways of knowing. All our various ways of knowing are founded and supported on the fact that God knows us. Knowing begins with God.

Week Twenty Five

Monday

I Don't Know

One of the great freedoms of Christianity is the freedom to say, "I don't know". People who don't have God's peace feel pressure to know everything and be right all the time. People feel shame in not knowing but the real shame is in pretending to know. We need to know Jesus, which isn't only an intellectual or rational way of knowing. You cannot seek wisdom unless you know you don't have it. Not many people are attracted to a know it all. The more you realize you don't know the faster you learn and gain wisdom.

Tuesday

Fundamentalism

Everyone is a fundamentalist and has foundation principles by which to understand the world and life. The fundamentals we claim and the fundamentals we live by are often different. It is fundamental to a humanist that people are good, to a post-modernist that people invent themselves, to a communist that equal distribution is more important than production, to a capitalist that freedom and funding are basic, to a Christian that Truth is revealed, to an atheist that Truth is not revealed but only discovered. What are the fundamentals of your life? Are you faithful to them or inconsistent?

Wednesday

"I Know What I Like."

Every life form knows what it likes. Most of our liking doesn't make sense and is not rational. We can pretend to like something because we are "supposed to like it". Not liking something doesn't mean we don't understand it or appreciate it. If someone likes something we don't, it doesn't make sense to us. They might not be able to tell us why they like it. To like is to enjoy or be attracted. We enjoy sin or we wouldn't do it. Liking tells us something about ourselves, not something about what we like.

Thursday

Strong and Weak

Each of us has strong points and weak points, strong fruits of the Spirit and weak ones. To strengthen what is already strong is natural. To strengthen what is weak is spiritual. God wants us to strengthen what is weak, so we become whole and holy people. If our knowledge is strong, we should strengthen our experience. If our experience is strong, we should strengthen our knowledge. Strengthening what is weak is a frightening move into the unknown. May God help us to walk by faith and hold the hand of Jesus. Amen.

Friday

Language II

God's Word is faithful and committed and worth keeping. Because we are made in His image our words should also be faithful and committed and worth keeping. It is no help to us if Jesus says, "Your sins are like forgiven or whatever…" We have a strong natural sense of an excessive freedom in our use of language (it is only words). The Holy Spirit gives us a spiritual sense of commitment and trustworthiness in language. It is a great battle to be faithful and careful with our language because our language sins have become habits. Take courage!

Week Twenty Six

Monday

Identity

Id-entity. Self-thing. This is not enough for life in God's Kingdom. The identity of Jesus is in His relationships with the Father and the Holy Spirit. Our identity is in our relationships with God and each other. True identity is larger than self. The image of God is them, not him or her. Identify yourself by love rather than a description of yourself. God, please help us to realize our identity is not in ourselves but in our relationships made possible and sustained by You. Amen.

Tuesday

Jesus is the Answer

Children in Sunday School learn that "Jesus" is a good guess in answering most questions. Actually, there is a great truth in that. The meaning of the Creation, the Flood, the Tower of Babel, the calling of Abraham and the history of the Jews, the Law of the Old Testament and human life in general is only in Jesus. When we understand Jesus we understand everything else. Jesus is the center of everything and gives everything meaning. The center is not a point or self-centered circle but a Cross and a Person – radiant and embracing.

Wednesday

Justice and Love

Justice and Love are very similar to each other. In the Bible "just" doesn't only mean fair or equal. It means fitting and appropriate. A justified angle fits the window frame. A justified person fits the frame of God's character and belongs with Him. Love is choosing to act into the loved one's life in ways that encourage and support their becoming who God wants them to be in His image. Justice and Love belong and work together. It is hard to imagine having one without the other. Jesus justifies us by His Love. Live like Jesus.

Thursday

Learning from Our Emotions

God made our emotions. They are precious and we learn a lot from them. They are also broken and twisted by sin and often lie to us. Our emotions teach us a great deal about ourselves – our appetites and tastes and fears and pleasures. Emotions and experiences are half of truth. The other half is fact and meaning, which are both independent of and complimentary to our emotions and experiences. To kill our emotions is to kill our-selves. To equate our emotions with God's Word and Truth is to know good and evil and die.

Friday

Limits of Freedom

My freedom to swing my fist ends at your nose. My freedom of speech ends at lying and slander. When we understand, and respect the forms of mechanics, physics and aerodynamics we become free to fly across the ocean. If we ignore or violate the forms, we crash. If we go outside the forms God gives us for life, we move toward death. We choose some limits. Some are made by God or the society we live in. If we try to live only within the limits we choose for our-selves we will destroy ourselves and others.

Week Twenty Seven

Monday

Deliver Us from Evil

There are no circumstances, nothing that happens to us and nothing we do that is not interesting to the devil. There is always opportunity for him to lead us astray toward death. We can resist the devil by turning to God for protection. If this is a constant practice and attitude on our part, God will keep us safe in his arms and give us freedom to live our lives undisturbed by evil. This will optimize the goodness of our imperfect choices. Everything about our lives is interesting to God. Turn to Hm. God is Love.

Tuesday

Our Brother's Keeper

Many Christians have been stressed under the weight of being their brother's keeper. God did not tell Cain he was his brother's keeper. Cain knew that only God can keep us, so he was cynically asking "Am I God to my brother?". Everyone makes their own responses and lives with the consequences. Our responsibility is to love our brother and pray God to keep them. We must care for each other, support and pray for each other, but not keep each other. We are not our brother's keeper – it is hard enough to be their brother.

Wednesday

Worry

We are commanded not to worry. This is hard because many things threaten, stress and confuse us. We want to know the future and it is hard to trust God about the unknown. When we worry about things, we often feel that we are being more responsible than when we say "no" to worry and trust God. When we trust, we have more energy and stability to be responsible. Wisdom is seeing the difference between things we can actually do something about and things we must passively trust God about. Pray for wisdom. God wants you to have it.

Thursday

Angels

The natural and supernatural parts of reality interface. Angels (Malachi) are messengers of God to people. People see angels in a variety of ways: fire, a voice, a person with or without wings. The supernatural works into the natural in unpredictable ways. Most people experience angels, sometimes without knowing it. Angels can manifest physically, influencing physical space and even eating with people. Angels bring the supernatural into the natural for teaching, warning, en-couragement, announcement. It is good to be receptive to the messengers of God. When you bring God's Word and Grace to people you serve like an angel.

Friday

Covenant

A covenant is like a job offer from the Owner of a company. The Owner offers belonging, protection, community, insurance, productive work, and retirement plan. The Owner gives Himself in ethical principles, which express Himself and gives us the work of spreading His Truth all over the world. Our part is to believe that the Owner and company are good and true and faith-fully commit ourselves to living within the company guidelines. Trying to live in the company by other principles won't work. We cannot keep the covenant perfectly, but Jesus has, and we can share in His perfection.

Week Twenty Eight

Monday

Trust and Confidence

In times of crises and stress like the Coronavirus pandemic of 2020, it is hard to trust. Governments make mistakes, anyone we meet might infect us, those who control our online life have various agendas. We cannot see or understand all details. But we can see the big picture in God's Person and pro-mises. He promises to keep us so nothing can separate us from Him. All the confusing and stressful details of our lives have their true meaning in the perspective of God's eternal promises. Keep your eyes on Jesus. Think about His power and faithfulness and be at peace.

Tuesday

Faith

Faith is the belief in the things we don't see or understand. Faith and knowledge work together and complement each other. We know we like chocolate by experience. We know 2+2=4 by observation and logic. We know we should stop at the red light by cultural tradition. We know our friend likes us by observation and faith. We know the Bible is true because it is accurate in history and science, it doesn't contradict itself and describes human life as we know it. We also know by faith and experience. Faith and science are friends. Taste and see.

Wednesday

Gratitude

One of the most common expressions toward God in the Bible is gratitude or thanksgiving. This is logical since we owe our existence and sustenance to Him. Gratitude is a rational and appropriate response and engagement in God's Reality. It is also an emotion, although not often recognized as that. The emotion of gratitude sweeps over us from time to time and should always be cultivated. Gratitude bathes our whole being with an atmosphere of health and well-being. Gratitude is the enemy of stress and anxiety. We don't imagine things to be grateful for. God's undeserved Grace is constant.

Thursday

Victory in Crises

In 2020 we are aware of our need for God to protect and heal us from the Corona Virus and its social and economic side effects. Let us bring our other areas in need of protection and healing to God: our tendency to worry, our groundless fears, our attitudes of prejudice and blame, giving a negative or paranoid interpretation to things people say and do, being a part of the problem instead of part of the solution. If we can be changed and healed in these and other ways, the time of corona will be a time of victory in our lives and relationships.

Friday

Love as Purpose

God gives us gifts of skill, ability and knowledge, prophecy, healing, discernment, tongues and fruits of patience, kindness, goodness, faithfulness, and gentleness. The purpose of all these is not to have them for themselves. They are given as tools that enable us to love. Love is not an emotion. Emotions happen to us and are not things we choose and do. Love is choosing and acting to encourage, enable and support others, building them up to be like Christ. By love we help people to be who God wants them to be. Love your neighbor as yourself.

Week Twenty Nine

Monday

What about those who have never heard?

Many tender-hearted Christians worry about those who have never heard the Gospel, read the Bible or met a missionary. The basic thing anyone needs to know to be saved is that they are broken and need God to forgive and fix them. God tells everyone this in various ways: The Bible, conscience, dreams, the Holy Spirit's conviction. The question is how people respond. In Romans 1 we read no one has an excuse. It is urgent to give people more opportunities to respond by missionary work near and far. Encourage poverty of spirit.

Tuesday

Male and Female

The idea that people are male, and female limits our freedom. The idea that gravity only pulls toward the earth also limits our freedom. Our limitations define and identify us as much as our possibilities do. If there are no limitations, there is no identity. The Bible says that God made His Image male and female as a default program. Biological and genetic science confirm the genetic polarity of animals. The Bible and Science agree. Gender is something that is given to us, not something we choose or invent. Imaginative gender alternatives are social or psychological constructs.

Wednesday

Your Brother's Keeper

When Cain had killed Abel, God asked him "Where is your brother Abel?" Cain answered "I don't know. Am I my brother's keeper?" This passage has often been used to put pressure on children to take responsibility for their siblings. The idea is that we should be and are our brother's keeper. But Cain was being cynical. He knew that God was his brother's keeper and meant "Am I God to my brother?" God is our keeper (Philippians 4:7). It is an unrealistic burden to be your brother's keeper. It is hard enough to be his brother.

Thursday

Our Basic Self

Many people struggle with "identity". Are we our abilities, our beauty, our handicaps, our jobs and careers, our wealth and possessions, our alpha nature, our victimhood? None of these things are finally adequate or stable. Our true and basic identity is beyond identity in the Will and Love of God before time began. God wills us to be in His Image in relationships with Him and others. Not "I think therefore I am" but "I am loved therefore I am". Don't struggle to invent yourself or "identify" as something. Be at peace and let God identify you.

Friday

Migration

1. We enter life through birth and live in a condition of death because of sin.

2. Then we can pass from death to life through belief in Jesus Christ.

3. Then we pass from life to death through natural death.

4. Then we pass from death to life with the appearing of Jesus and the restoration of everything.

Every-one goes through phases 1 and 3. Phases 2 and 4 are open options provided by God. Some decline phases 2 and 4, which is very sad. Where are you in this process? Be sure not to skip any of the phases.

Week Thirty

Monday

The Mind of Christ

The mind is a mysterious element of the self that, among other activities and in the case of humans, uses the brain as a tool to observe and understand reality. We see reality in episodes or linearly and narratively, projecting our experience as reality or experiencing and participating in a reality that is given to us. The Mind of Christ is full, comprehensive, objective and subjective, temporal and eternal. The eye of the Mind of Christ is "single" or holistic so that our whole bodies are full of light. Pray to have the Mind of Christ.

Tuesday

Mistrust

Trust is precious, powerful and fragile. Trusting God is foundational to the Christian Faith and life. The devil is constantly attacking trust to destroy it. He says, "Has God said?" "Make these stones into bread". "Jump off a building and make God prove Himself trustworthy." The thing to pray and work against during the Covid virus pandemic is the mushrooming of mistrust. Trust is the foundation of societies and economies. A threat against trust is a grave danger for all of us. Make an effort to be trustworthy in what you do and say. Be part of the solution.

Wednesday

In the Clouds in the Air

"After that, we who are still alive and are left will be caught up together with them in the clouds to meet the Lord in the air. And so we will be with the Lord forever." The "clouds" are not water vapor. They are the glory of God and His Kingdom, coming to earth with Jesus when He appears, answering the prayer "Your Kingdom come, Your Will be done on earth as it is in heaven". "So" means in the Cloud of the presence and glory of God – forever on the earth.

Thursday

Nothing is Safe

The woman's highest priority was safety and security. She thought her job was secure but saw people around her losing theirs. She thought her bank was safe but read about scandals and failures. She thought her Church was safe, but people fought and gossiped and competed. She thought her health and life insurance policies were secure but there were complications. She felt horribly that nothing and no one could be trusted. Then she remembered that Jesus had proven His trustworthiness by dying for her and promised to be with her always. Standing on this foundation she could face everything else.

Friday

Parable of a victim

Once upon a time there was a man who had various personal and business difficulties. He had been taught that he was a victim and had rights and entitlements. He wondered why God didn't give him what he deserved. The idea that he might be guilty of anything seemed an intolerable burden of debt. Then he realized that he could afford to be guilty because Jesus had already paid for every-thing. He could face his own responsibility for his life freely and realistically, knowing the weight of any amount of guilt could be lifted from him. The healing began.

Week Thirty One

Monday

People are Good

We need goodness in our lives and in our world. This prompts people to declare and believe they and other people are good. This is a dangerous fantasy, like declaring that poisonous snakes are safe. If people are good, they don't need Jesus, which is a terrible, deadly lie. We need perfect and absolute goodness. Sadly, people are not good enough, but happily God is. Only God is good and the measure of goodness, not our taste, pleasure or comfort. Because God is all good and all powerful, He can make us good if we let Him.

Tuesday

A.C.T.S.

Acts is the fifth book in the New Testament. It is also a useful guide to prayer:

A. – Adoration. As in many prayers in the Bible, it is good to begin prayer with praising or adoring God.

C. – Confession. It is good to confess our sins to God for renewing our justification and clearing ourselves for a better communication with Him.

T. – Thanksgiving. We have much to be thankful for. It is good and healthy to remember God's goodness and kindness to us and be thankful.

S. – Supplication. Finally, we can ask for anything that is in God Will.

Wednesday

Personal Goodness

In our day humanists teach us that we should value our natural goodness and have self-respect. The Apostle Paul teaches us that our goodness or righteousness is like filthy rags. True goodness is available to us from Jesus Christ. We can be truly good in Him and have realistic hope and joy and thankfulness. Goodness and life do not come from the natural created world or from our natural selves but from the Creator. If we are humble and poor in spirit, we can receive all we need for goodness and life from Jesus. Trust in Him and be glad.

Thursday

Let your eye be single

In Matthew 6:19-24 Jesus gave two examples of a divided reality: Storing up treasure on earth or in heaven and serving two masters, God or money. In between these examples is the solution to the problem. If your eye is single, if you see reality as a whole, held together by the power of the Word of Jesus, instead of divided, you will be full of light. If your eye is evil you will see reality as divided and in conflict. May God help us to see a reality unified in His Truth and Love. Amen.

Friday

Prayer and Bicycle Riding

Once there was a teenager who read lots of books and websites about bicycle riding. They felt that they knew all about it. One day they got on a friends' bicycle to ride it and fell off. They realized true knowledge involves doing. Later they read lots of books and websites about praying and loving their neighbors and felt they knew a lot about it. They started a blog about prayer and many people joined the discussion. They began to feel lonely and isolated and realized they needed to actually pray and love people in person.

Week Thirty Two

Monday

Predestination

God makes choices in eternity that effect all of time. He sees and knows time from the beginning to the end because He made it. He has known all of us since before we were born. His foreknowledge and predestination work together. We make choices in time and are always invited to choose God. From the perspective of time we can always live in hope. We know that God has chosen or predestined us when we choose Him, which we could not do without His help and personal calling. If we choose Him, He will accept us. Choose God.

Tuesday

Justice and Mercy

Justice by itself means to have what is fair or equal. People think of it as getting what they deserve. This is actually not so positive because if we are sinners what we deserve is death. People are interested in having their rights. If we are sinners, what are our rights? Our only right is to die because the wages of sin is death. Wonderfully, God does not offer us justice or our rights. He offers us mercy and life. Anyone who thinks they deserve salvation probably won't get it. Be poor in spirit and trust God.

Wednesday

Focus

Many things, people and circumstances invite (tempt) us to concentrate on them. Some urgent things fill the whole screen of our awareness and blot out most else. When our attention is centered on a particular need, fear or hope the picture is always out of focus and distorted. When our attention is centered on Jesus all the particular things come into clear focus. Jesus gives clear meaning and purpose to everything in our lives. If we focus on His Word as on a light at the end of a dark tunnel we know where we are and where we are going.

Thursday

Theology

Theology is the study of God. We need theologians to study, interpret and apply God's Word so we know how to live in His Kingdom. Often theology becomes the study of other theologians. It can get academically disconnected from ordinary life. God is Love. If the study of theology does not lead to greater love of God and other people, it has lost its way. The goal and focus of theological studies must always be the love of God and our neighbors.

Friday

Trust

Only God is fully trustworthy and only in His actual character and promises. Our imagination is not trustworthy. Everything and everyone betrays us in small and big ways, so we are wounded and handicapped. Much mental illness is an inability to trust. Being trustworthy is a way of being salt and light in the world. Trust is fragile and easily damaged. Trust in God is healing. When we are consistently faithful in what we say and do we add to the social capital of our culture. Trust is part of the Kingdom of God. Pray and work for it.

Week Thirty Three

Monday

The Least Faith

People become Christians because of many reasons, emotions and circumstances. One reason for believing Christianity is that it takes less faith to believe in it than to believe in anything else. Faith is needed but faith like a mustard seed, not faith like a coconut. Our faith can be small but living and growing and bearing fruit because Christianity gives clear answers to more questions than other faith systems. It takes more faith to believe that people are good or evolution or communism or rationalism or materialism or astrology. Choose the rational faith. Choose Christianity.

Tuesday

Reading and Listening

It is very difficult to read or listen clearly because our own expectations and assumptions muddy the waters. When people speak and we basically hear ourselves, conversation is impossible, and we end up lonely and alienated. When we read into a text instead of out of it, we also end up talking with ourselves. Love is other centered. If we sacrifice our agendas and concentrate on the other, understanding will grow and both of us will be blessed. We don't need to agree with what we hear or read but we need to look away from ourselves.

Wednesday

Forgiveness

Forgive means to "give for", to pay for something someone else owes. If someone hurts us or gossips about us, they cannot possibly pay the debt. The only possibility is that we pay it for them, drawing on the Bank of Jesus, Who paid everything for everyone. It is thought to be therapeutic to forgive to separate from a negative tie. This is not Christian forgiveness. We don't need Jesus to forgive us in order to separate from us. Forgiveness is for healing and restoration of relationships. True forgiveness is impossible without faith in God, Who makes forgiveness possible.

Thursday

Investing in Prayer

Normally, investment always involves risk, whether we invest in companies or personal relationships. In prayer there is a risk that we won't get what we want or become confused. But there is no risk that God will not bless us and make our lives more real when we pray. Prayer is treasure. Where our treasure is our hearts are also. When we invest in other people by praying for them our heart attitudes toward them change because we have invested in them. Try praying for people who are difficult or annoy you and see what happens.

Friday

Needy

There once was a man who was a Christian and knew a lot about Christianity. He had ups and downs in life and brought them all to God in prayer. One day he was struck by a heavy depression that weighed him down and made him hopeless and cynical. He cried out to God in his desperate and confused need. Gradually he experienced that his desperate need was poverty of spirit. The more he realized his poverty of spirit, the more of the Kingdom of God he had in his life. God can use anything to bless His children.

Week Thirty Four

Monday

Absolute Evil

People often speak of "Absolute Evil". Actually, evil is never absolute. Good is absolute. God is Good and eternal. Evil came into being by God's creatures and only exists as a contrast to good. Good exists independently of evil but evil is dependent on Good. Evil is a distorted parenthesis in the eternal sentence of Good. Good is original and absolute while evil is derivative and relative. Evil is destructive in time. If we trust in God we are delivered from evil in eternity. Good conquers evil and swallows it up in victory so it will be no more.

Tuesday

Test Everything

In I Thessalonians Paul teaches us to test everything in order to avoid putting out the Spirit's fire and holding prophecies in con-tempt. If we only say "yes" to everything that claims to be a prophecy and every emotion and experience that comes to us, we go out of focus with God's Truth. The result of testing should be first holding on to all that is good so we can identify what is evil. If we test to identify evil, it will not help us to know the good. The purpose of testing is to increase our love.

Wednesday

The Problem of Good

If God is all powerful and all good, why is there evil in the world? If it were not for the goodness of God, we wouldn't know what evil is. Everything would just be normal and natural like volcanoes, beautiful sunsets, and poisonous snakes. A more useful question is: If everything is cooling down and tending toward chaos, why is there good? Nature is not good or bad – it just is what it is. Good and evil are supernatural energies working into nature. Good is original, beginning with God. Evil is a distortion which God is correcting.

Thursday

Fig Leaves

When Adam and Eve decided to know good and evil for themselves rather than depending on God for this knowledge, they discovered they were naked and vulnerable. Instead of turning to the Creator for a solution they reached into the creation and got fig leaves to conceal and protect themselves. This is like putting a band aid on a cancer. People have been doing the same thing ever since. What are your fig leaves? Think and pray about abandoning them and turning to your Creator, Who can hide you in Christ and protect you from alienation and death.

Friday

Naming

In the process of creation, God made divisions or categories and named them; day/night, earth/sea, sun/moon. Then, when he divided people, made in His Image, from the rest of creation, He told them to continue the naming process, beginning with the animals. Naming establishes dominion and ownership. People name animals and plants. Animals and plants do not name people. God is faithful to His Own Name and to the names He gives. Evil distorts and confuses the names. We must not name ourselves but receive the name God gives us. We must be faithful to the names we give.

Week Thirty Five

Monday

Strong Experiences

Many of us have some strong experiences of a landscape, an animal or a supernatural presence. These experiences are often strongly emotional. If the experience and emotions give us love for other people and the world and motivate us to serve, they are probably from God. We should act on them and keep them as inspiring memories. If the experiences are mostly about ourselves, they are still very pleasant and strong but might be from our metabolism or memories or psychosomatically caused. They can also be temptations to center on ourselves. We should stay awake and test everything.

Tuesday

Pride

Why is the Bible so negative about pride? It is good and healthy to be pleased and encouraged by our abilities and accomplishments. Pride can be shallow, like pride in my eye color or skin texture, which are not abilities or accomplishments. Pride can be vain, which means empty or worthless. It is natural to be proud, while it is spiritual to be thankful. Pride in others can be good but a person who "is proud" is self-centered, self-dependent and imploding. The devil is proud and dead and wants us to be too. Jesus is humble and powerfully alive.

Wednesday

Thankfulness

True thankfulness requires humility and poverty of spirit. Thankfulness to God is infinite because when we are thankful for being thankful an upward spiral begins. Thankfulness is always appropriate to God and often to others. If we remember what to be thankful for it puts the other things in perspective with God's Grace. We need to think about bad things in order to resist and forgive. Being thankful refreshes and energizes us and is therapeutic. A small investment in being thankful pays a big dividend in blessing. Make thankfulness, especially in hard times, a joyful discipline in your life.

Thursday

Truth and Mercy

Some people are tempted by the hope of improving relationships by telling the whole truth. Being fully open and not hiding can feel purifying. But God's Truth is not facts alone. Truth only brings life when it works with Love and Mercy. If the way you blow your nose truly disgusts me, I might choose in mercy not to tell you. The way Truth and Mercy work together is mysterious. We need God's Wisdom to make the best imperfect choice. God help us to be slow to speak and quick to pray. Amen.

Friday

Questions as Blessings

When talking to unbelieving friends and relatives about Jesus, Christians often make statements and recount experiences. While these can be true it is easy to say "no" to them. It is harder to say "no" to a question. Questions go under the radar and give the Holy Spirit an entrance to work in the person's mind and heart. Ask questions about meaning, purpose, identity as a gift and give space for thought. When people begin to ask you back, preach Christ because they are hungry. Questions stimulate appetite. Pray for effective questions to ask. Love your neighbors.

Week Thirty Six

Monday

Earth, Air, Fire and Water

God loves the Earth and made us from it. The risen body of Jesus could be touched; it ate and worked. Through the Air comes the Wind of the Spirit, Who points us to Jesus, teaches us and gives us holy fruit. The breath of God gives us life. Fire is for clean-sing, revealing or destruction. Fire shows the needle in the haystack of our sins. Water destroyed the earth once and now cleanses and refreshes us. Our God is sovereign over Earth, Air, Fire and Water and uses them to work His Will.

Tuesday

Race

Race doesn't seem to be a factor in the Kingdom of God. God loves everyone. Everyone needs God. God seems to be color blind. God is the great leveler: The rich are poor; the poor are rich. Color, family history, education, religious background, political views, entitlements, or privileges don't seem to make much difference. We are not saved or lost by our background, only our fore-ground. We are all the same to Jesus. To think differently causes problems. Healing can be painful and frightening. Let us allow the Holy Spirit to form this understanding in our hearts and minds.

Wednesday

Relevant

Is the Bible relevant to our culture and society? This question assumes that our culture and society are the measure of truth and reality and wonders if the Bible can be made to fit in. Christianity is radical and assumes that the Bible describes truth and reality. The values of the Bible are absolute and eternal, while alternative values of any human culture are relative and temporary. If the Bible is true, we should measure our culture against it, not the other way around. Are your personal and social cultures relevant to the Kingdom of God? Think about it.

Thursday

Religion or Idolatry

Over time, Christians have developed various ways of responding to God's salvation, which we can call religion. These include architecture, liturgies, rites, ceremonies, traditions, paintings, sculptures, windows, special clothing, creeds, catechisms, music, and other things. God is Love. The Gospel of Jesus Christ is Love. We need to think and pray about how all our religious practices direct and support us in loving each other. If they do, they are a blessing for us. If they don't, they can be a distracting idolatry or escape. Don't abandon religion but make sure it is actually a blessing for you.

Friday

Mother's Day

This should be a lifestyle, not an event. One of the 10 commandments says, "Honor your father and mother.". This does not mean obey as some think. Obeying a senile or demented parent doesn't help anyone. To honor means to respect the life; to support, protect and preserve the life. This is why the commandment is connected to the promise; "so that you will live long.". If your children see you honoring the lives of your parents they will honor your life. Parents can reasonably include other older people, which will increase the social capital and blessing of a nation greatly.

Week Thirty Seven

Monday

Religion

Religion is either a system of activities intended to connect a person with absolute truth or a faithful devotion to some basic principles (like communism). It usually in-volves the supernatural. The basis of Christianity is God connecting Himself with us through His Word in the creation, the incarnation of Jesus Christ, the Bible and the activity of the Holy Spirit. Christianity starts with God coming to us, not us trying to reach God, so it is different from religion. It all starts with God's Love. It doesn't start with our efforts or system. Let yourself be found by God.

Tuesday

Ascension Day

On Ascension Day we remember that Jesus was taken up and a cloud hid Him. This cloud was not water vapor but the Shekinah Glory of God. Jesus went into dimensions of reality which we cannot see but He did not go far away. He had said two things that fit together: "I am going away." and "I am always with you.". Heaven is the supernatural dimensions of reality, which are in the same place as the natural dimensions like height is in the same place as length and width. Jesus is ascended and right here with us. May God use the presence of Jesus to comfort and challenge us. Amen.

Wednesday

Revelation

Some of the events in the book of Revelation take place on earth and some in heaven (the supernatural dimensions of reality). The ones on earth take place in time, while the ones in heaven take place in eternity. "A day is like a thousand years and a thousand years is like a day" describes the relationship between time and eternity. Can we expect to measure the events in heaven with a calendar? Probably not. The events are true and real even though we cannot fully imagine or measure them. We live by faith and not by sight.

Thursday

The Chorus of Ecclesiastes

A man can do nothing better than to eat and drink and find satisfaction in his work. 2:24-25.

Then I realized that it is good and proper for a man to eat and drink, and to find satisfaction in his toilsome labor under the sun during the few days of life God has given him. 5:18.

I commend the enjoyment of life, because nothing is better for a man under the sun, than to eat and drink and be glad. 8:15.

Go, eat your food with gladness, and drink your wine with a joyful heart. 9:7.

Friday

Righteousness

A "right angle" (90 degrees) is right because it fits into the window or door frame. Be-coming righteous is being reshaped to fit into God's Kingdom and become more in His Image. We should work in obedience to become more fitting. This is the small part of the process of becoming righteous. The big part is God's part in giving us a new heart and a right spirit, cleaning us from the distortions of sin by the blood of Jesus and guiding and encouraging us by His Holy Spirit. Trust in God's part so you can do your part better.

Week Thirty Eight

Monday

Risk and Trust

The wealth of nations and all good relation-ships are built on trust. With trust there is usually risk: The stock might crash, the company might downsize, the spouse die, the friend change, the Church split. It is good to analyze the risks and be realistic about our hopes and expectations. We can dare to trust and risk if our lives are founded and framed by the promises of God to save and keep us. In this there is zero risk. God will not die or fail or change. Live in focus with the one risk free relationship.

Tuesday

Miracles

A miracle is a specific incident of the supernatural acting into the natural world. Miracles can be rationally understood if we include the supernatural in our worldview. They cannot be scientifically explained. Miracles are not natural. We can think of a localized pocket of negative entropy. Some miracles are constant like the working of the Holy Spirit in your life or God keeping you through all kinds of experiences and circumstances. Some miracles are specific like healing or striking a border guard going blind for a moment. The Christian always lives with general and specific miracles. Be thankfully awake.

Wednesday

Traditions

Traditions are essential for remembering God's saving history and identifying ourselves in the flow of history that is larger than our moment. Artistic and cultural expressions happen in traditions. If traditions take first place in our hearts, they can replace the love of God and neighbor and become idols. The Holy Spirit can help us love and profit from our traditions without worshiping them and despising others. Traditions should serve Christ and His Love for the whole world. Christ is not contained in our traditions. Let us humble ourselves so our hearts and minds can be guarded in Christ Jesus our Lord.

Thursday

Tithing

90% is greater than 100%. This equation does not make sense in the world's economy. In the economy of the Kingdom of God it makes perfect sense. Our wealth is not only money, but also time, skill, expertise, hospitality, and wisdom. We love and serve God by loving and serving other people. We can be creative with our tithing, not giving it all to an organization for other people to manage. Tithing makes us more careful and thankful about our resources. Tithing makes friends, builds community, and invests in social capitol. Try it and see what God will do.

Friday

Self-Referential

Self-Referential is often thought of as a positive value, especially in art. Actually, self-referential is another way of saying sin and death. God is absolutely and eternally other referential. The reference of Jesus is not Himself but the Father and the Spirit. Adam and Eve were made other referential. Their references were God and each other. They became self-referential by knowing good and evil for themselves, independently. God is Love. Love is other-referential. Life is only in God and Love. Allow the Holy Spirit to make you more and more other-referential and receive more and more life from God.

Week Thirty Nine

Monday

Spiritual Activities

The resurrected and glorified Jesus Christ is our only example of the true spiritual life. What did He do? He ate and drank (Luke 24:36-44, Acts 1:4). He taught history (Luke 24:13-27). He worked, created and practiced hospitality (John 21:4-13). Eating, drinking, teaching, working, being creative and practicing hospitality are all spiritual activities for the Christian. Natural activities become spiritual by connection with the supernatural through prayer, thankfulness and God's blessing. The religious or ceremonial part of our spiritual lives belongs with the other parts, which are equally real and spiritual. Spiritual means totally real, healed, not divided.

Tuesday

"Spiritual" Connections

Many people ask and wonder if various events and circumstances have a "spiritual" or supernatural connection. Two questions might help think this through: Is there anything that you do or that happens to you that God is not interested in? Is there anything that you do or that happens to you that the devil is not interested in? We are connected with the supernatural part of reality 24/7. Prayer is always indicated. We don't need to be in vague confusion or worry. We are always in a battle and should always include God in our situation. Pray constantly.

Wednesday

Your Kingdom Come, Your Will Be Done

The Kingdom of God is not the Church or in another place. Jesus said the Kingdom is coming, near, here, among us and inside us. The Kingdom of God is the Will of God. We need His Will in our hearts, our relationships, our communities and in our world. We cannot do much about wars and weather and elections, but we can pray for God's Name to be hallowed or known as Holy, and for His Kingdom to come, His Will be done on earth now. Jesus taught us to pray like that.

Thursday

Victorious Life

Sometimes we are disappointed and discouraged because we are not overcoming various ungodly habits of action and attitude. We are alarmed because we are not increasing in holiness and victory. The real source of our salvation is not in our effort but God's Grace in Jesus Christ. Often God is at work in us in ways we don't see. Check for growth in the fruits of the Spirit. When you find an increase in love, joy, peace, patience, kindness, goodness, faithfulness, gentleness or self-control you will know that God is at work in you and be encouraged to make your own effort.

Friday

Testing and Tempting

Testing (Dokimazo in Greek) looks for the good. Tempting (Peirazo in Greek) looks for the bad. Sometimes these words are translated in the same way. God is always testing us to prove and demonstrate that our faith is strong and that we have grown as His children. We should test each other to find out what is good. We are tempted to tempt each other to find out what is bad, so we feel better. Show people how good they are and encourage them to be better with God's help. Build people up, don't tear them down.

Week Forty

Monday

The Desires of Our Hearts

"Delight yourself in the Lord and He will give you the desires of your heart." Ps. 37:4. "Earth has nothing I desire besides you." Ps. 73:25. This is a very great promise. There is a lot of discussion about which desires of our hearts we can expect to get from God. The text makes it obvious. What we desire is what we delight in, so God is promising to give us Himself. If we get little and have God, we are rich. If we get much and don't have God, we are poor. Treasure God.

Tuesday

Pray For Your Enemies

When people frustrate, oppose, betray, attack or gossip, we are wounded and perhaps scarred. It can damage our ability to trust and cripple our relationships with others. Prayer is a powerful life tool is such situations. When we pray for our enemies we take the higher ground of power and authority. Our enemies are wounded and damaged people. We have the power to call down God's healing blessing on them. This changes our perspective radically. Prayer changes us from being victims to being change agents. Pray for your enemies. Bless those who curse you. Try it.

Wednesday

The End is Near!

Many Christians are interested in and concerned about the End Times. People ask, "Are we in the End Times?" Yes, we are, ever since John wrote Revelation. He also wrote that we are in the "Last Hour" 2000 years ago. The End of the world is near! "End" doesn't mean "finish" but fulfillment or reaching the goal. God will bring the world or earth to the fulfillment of His purpose in creating it. The End is near actually means the Beginning is near – the Beginning of the fulfillment of God's Kingdom on earth. Your Kingdom come!

Thursday

The End Times

People often ask "Do you think we are in the End Times?" I John 2:18 says "This is the last hour", so the answer is "yes". An hour of eternity is long by our standards. In Acts 1:6-7 the disciples wanted to know if the end or restoration was "now". Jesus "It is not for you to know." God does not want us to know when the end will be. He doesn't want us to calculate, chart and graph and argue about it. He wants us to trust Him, live as he wants and to be prepared.

Friday

The Parable of the Mother and the Boy

Once upon a time there was a woman who had a little boy. She loved the boy and knew that he would touch the hot stove in the kitchen. She begged and scolded him and pleaded with him not to touch the stove. When he did touch the stove one day it was not her fault. She hurt for him. Her know-ledge that he would touch the stove did not take away his significance and responsibility. When the boy was sorry he had dis-obeyed his mother, she kissed him and forgave him.

Week Forty One

Monday

Humility and Meekness

Many think of meekness or humility as shyness, always sitting in the back row or being a doormat. Moses was the leader of over a million people and opposed Pharaoh to his face, yet he was "the meekest man alive". When Moses told God he wasn't the right man to lead Israel he was being proud. When he accepted the leadership he was being humble. Meekness is realism about our weak unworthiness and acceptance of what God gives us to do. Meekness is following God rather than our own imagination, fears and desires. The meek will inherit the earth.

Tuesday

The Problem of Evil

If God is all good and all powerful, why is there evil? This question cannot be answered unless people are assumed to be responsible change agents. God didn't make us automatically good, but with the responsibility of choosing good. Often, we don't, and evil happens. History is linear and accumulative. Evil builds up and effects everyone. We are not guilty of what happens to us, only of what we choose and do. People tend to think of evil as "them". If God would do something to get rid of all evil, what would happen to you?

Wednesday

Loving Our Neighbor is Loving God

Once upon a time there was someone who believed in God and wanted to love Him. So, they began to read the Bible and go to Church and practice religious disciplines. They were militantly zealous for God's Truth, talking about it a lot and correcting anyone who had any misunderstanding. They tried hard to be a model of religious uprightness. But there was a hollow place in their heart. Then they began to love God by loving and serving their neighbors and the hollow place was filled up with deep, quiet, and energizing joy.

Thursday

Anger and Paranoia

Many of us are troubled with attacks of angry and paranoid thoughts and feelings which are only partly rational. These can fill our mind with a dark or fiery cloud that makes life miserable and lonely. These thoughts are never loving or productive. It is wrong, although very tempting, to follow these thoughts and develop them. We are forbidden to worry about this. We can wear ourselves out with the struggle. Why not do something instead? Bring them to Jesus and let Him do something. He will protect, heal, forgive, comfort and accept you. Try it. God bless you.

Friday

The Spirit Blows and Hovers

"Spirit" means "wind" in Hebrew and Greek in the Bible. The Wind is a Person with a Will and a Purpose. The Wind hovers like a dove over the waters of creation, the flood and the baptism of Jesus – three new beginnings. The Wind blows and breathes into us Truth, Wisdom, rebuke, guidance, comfort and the Name of Jesus. He is the Spirit of Jesus Christ, proclaiming Him and pointing to Him as our Savior and Guide in life. The Spirit enters into us, plants seeds and bears fruit. We should treasure and love Him more.

Week Forty Two

Monday

Test the Message, not the Messenger

The Apostle Paul was not good looking and did not make everyone feel good about themselves all the time. Some false teachers looked great, had good references, were polished speakers and flattered the people. Many were confused and led astray. It is still a danger to get caught in the looks, personality, acting skills and popularity of a teacher in Church, school, politics, the arts or advertising and believe their message without testing it. Everyone knows how they feel about a message. Only those with the mind of Christ know how they think.

Tuesday

Time and Eternity

A matrix is an atmosphere in which things happen. Water is the matrix of tea, air is the matrix of sound, cyberspace is the matrix of emails. The matrix of things happening in space is time. The matrix of things happening outside of space is eternity. Eternity is not infinite time. It is a separate matrix. Every point of time is present to every point of eternity. This is why prophecy is possible. We can connect with eternity through prayer and other means. When Jesus appears time and eternity will conflate in God's Kingdom on the new earth. May God help us to see from His perspective of eternity. Amen.

Wednesday

The Temple of the Holy Spirit

God is the God of relationships and not self-centered. He wants us to be the same in His Image. The temple of the Holy Spirit and the body of the bride of Christ are not about us as individuals but about us as a family or community, children of God together. Where two or more are together Christ and His Spirit are present in a more complete way than when we are alone. We can pray alone, and the Spirit blesses us individually, but our eternal life is not singular. Practice now for eternity.

Thursday

Postmodern 10 Commandments

(continued from page 52)

VI. Thou shalt accept any collateral damage from the project of thy life.

VII. Thou shalt never be unfaithful to thy own feelings and desires.

VIII. Thou shalt appropriate anything thou canst get away with.

IX. Thou shalt shape truth to serve thyself or whatever.

X. Thou shalt not desire to appropriate any value that cometh not from thine inner self.

Friday

Trust and Panic

Christians live in a peaceful atmosphere of trust because of the faithful power of God our savior. We do not live in a paranoid miasma of conspiracy panic. All authority comes from God but is never used perfectly. Governments make mistakes. We are to be wise as serpents and gentle as doves. We are to give God what is God's and give Caesar what is Caesar's. We are not to condemn each other for drawing the line in different places. Christians are to bless the city so that it will be a blessing to live in it.

Week Forty Three

Monday

Two Kinds of People

There are only two kinds of people on the earth – those who know their need of God (the poor in spirit) and those who don't (the rich in spirit). The rich depend on them-selves, their careers and accomplishments, their societies and traditions for their identity and meaning. The poor depend on God in Christ. Both groups include wealthy and poor, attractive and unattractive, admirable and despised, religious and less religious, healthy and sick, beautiful and ugly. We tend to judge by appearances and our taste. God judges by the heart. Be poor in spirit and live.

Tuesday

Unanswered Prayer

Many Christians consider a prayer unanswered if they don't get what they want. "Yes" is not the only possible answer from God. He might say "yes", "no", "maybe" or "wait". All of these are answers. Jesus said if a child asks us for a fish, we won't give them a snake, or a stone instead of bread. We don't know what we really need and sometimes ask God for a snake or a stone. Because He loves us, He doesn't give us those things. Praying in Jesus' Name means asking for what God wants, not what we want.

Wednesday

Comfort

The comfort of God doesn't basically mean being warm and dry, well fed and healthy with a secure job. It is more that our sins are forgiven, we are acceptable to God and He keeps us and holds us in His arms by his gentle power. We all have various troubles and anxieties. It is wise to ask God for His comfort and give ourselves to his embrace like the prodigal son. God wants to comfort us. If we ask for it, we know we will receive it because it is what He wants. Stay close and trust God.

Thursday

Unconditional Love

Emotions change under different internal and external conditions. Love is much bigger than emotions. Love is the choosing to act and be available to support the loved one in becoming who God wants them to be. God is constantly and perfectly available and acting to make us truly in His image. The effectiveness of God's Love and our love depends on the condition of the loved one's willingness to accept it. Emotions can support or inhibit true love. Love is not something that happens to us. It is something we choose. Work to choose love under all conditions.

Friday

Treasure Inside and Out

We store up treasure in heaven by blessing others and making their lives more beautiful and real. Blessing others can become an industry on the outside, while inside we are rotting away. When Christian leaders crash and burn people sometimes say, "Their work was a blessing to me.", but the Christian leader was not blessed. We should not only work to help others but should make sure we are also being fed and nourished. Be ready to receive God's healing and guidance. Be ready to change on the inside as well as bless on the outside.

Week Forty Four

Monday

Understanding God's Word

Language is difficult. It is probably im-possible to describe with words in space and time things and events that take place mostly in eternity. There are three heavens: where the birds fly, where the stars turn and the supernatural. One word is used for all of them. The text itself doesn't say enough – it needs to be explained. Precision is limited and never perfect. If we needed more precision, God would give it to us. We cannot understand God's Word adequately only with our mind. God's Word is the Bible, the creation and Jesus. True understanding is a holistic relationship.

Tuesday

Value and Desire

Desire increases perceived value immediately. Where your heart is, there will be your treasure also. You will invest yourself in what you want. We can follow the natural desires that come and go, or we can learn to desire what God desires for us and be stable in His Truth and Love. If we want what God wants all our other desires and values come into their proper place and focus. With us this is impossible, but we can ask God to help us want what He wants, and He will do it. Desire what God desires.

Wednesday

Victory During Covid

Not all things are good. In all things God works for good for those who love Him. Let's look for and receive God's victory in our lives during Covid. Because of the restrictions, does the Holy Spirit teach you to treasure and develop relationships? Does He teach you patience, faithfulness and kindness? The Covid pandemic will end. God's victories in our lives will not end. Rejoice! We can ask God to end the virus. God does not give us everything we want. He gives us everything He wants, which is much better. Love God and let Him love you.

Thursday

Wanting What God Wants

God has promised that if we ask for what He wants us to have He will give it to us. It is clear God wants us and everyone to grow in the fruits of the Spirit and the values of the Beatitudes and to love each other. It is not clear God wants us to be healed or get the job or the visa or pass the test. What else do we know from Scripture that God wants for us and others? Ask for what God wants and everything else will come into focus in His Kingdom.

Friday

What About Those Who Have Never Heard? (Part 1)

Many tender-hearted Christians worry about those who have never heard the Gospel, read the Bible or met a missionary. The basic thing anyone needs to know to be saved is that they are broken and need God to forgive and fix them. God tells everyone this in various ways: The Bible, conscience, dreams, the Holy Spirit's conviction. The question is how people respond. In Romans 1 we read no one has an excuse. It is urgent to give people more opportunities to respond by missionary work near and far. Encourage poverty of spirit.

Week Forty Five

Monday

Cause and Effect

God made the universe with a law of cause and effect and sustains that law. If a Chris-tian and a non-Christian jump off a building they will both fall down, not up. If you make your own morals and identity (eat from the fruit of the tree of the knowledge of good and evil), you will die. When people expe-rience the consequences of their choices the Bible often says, "God did it." because cause and effect are from Him. Our participation in history and responsibility for our actions are not eliminated by God sustaining cause and effect.

Tuesday

What About Those Who Have Never Heard? (Part II)

Knowing that we need God is essential for salvation. Anyone who knows this and reaches out to God will be saved. Having a Bible and hearing the Gospel is not enough. God has various ways of letting people know they need Him: The Bible, other people, the creation that shows how inconsistent and unfaithful we are, conviction by the Holy Spirit. God does not control peoples' response. Some reject Him, though God tells everyone they need Him. It is important that they hear about God's Truth and Love through Jesus Christ from us.

Wednesday

Love and Trust

God loves us and we can trust Him for all he has actually promised but not for what we have imagined. The effect of God's love for us depends on our receiving it. We must always love our neighbors. Trust is different. Everyone is broken and distorted by their sin and that of others. We must trust others in hope and within the limits of their brokenness. We must not expect too much. If someone is kleptomaniac, we should love them and not trust them to overcome the disease immediately. Unwise trust can make things worse.

Thursday

Why?

"Why?" is often a very agonized cry. Why me? Why this? Why now? We want to have a cause and effect understanding. When people asked Jesus, in John 9, why a man was born blind He basically said "don't look back for a reason, look forward for a purpose." We put ourselves more in focus with God's Kingdom and purpose when we ask "How will God use this for good in the lives of those who love Him?" "Why?" can be an expression of hopelessness because we know we won't find out. "What for?" ex-presses hope and trust.

Friday

Wisdom

Once there was a very intelligent, educated and gifted pastor. He knew the Bible and could teach it well. The Church profited from his work and service. One day he welcomed an older woman into the Church. She was not very intelligent or educated or skilled. She spent much of her time praying for people, encouraging and helping them as she could. Through fellowship with this woman, the pastor also became gradually more wise by her example and encourage-ment. Intelligence has value but without wisdom, not full value. Wisdom without intelligence has full value. We learn from each other.

Week Forty Six

Monday

90% >100%

"90% is greater than 100%" is not a true equation in space time mathematics. It is wonderfully true in the Kingdom of God. Tithing is not commanded in the New Testament but giving generously and cheerfully is. Setting aside 10% of our income (gross or net) for giving away, regularly or spontaneously, is an eternal investment for us. It also seems mysteriously to bring Peace and financial security here and now. Many Christians are afraid to do this because their faith is weak. Don't think of it as a sacrifice. Think of it as an investment. Try it.

Tuesday

Cyberspace

Cyberspace is a bit mysterious to most of us. So is the Supernatural part of reality. Life is hard and dangerous. Death is easy. Safety is not available in the physical world, cyber-space or the supernatural in themselves. We only find safety in Jesus and He is with us everywhere. When we spend time in Cyber-space (whatever that actually means) we need to remember Jesus, stay close to Him and include Him in our activities. We are always in God's presence and should not think of taking a break. We don't want God to take a break from us!

Wednesday

Words and Feelings

Once upon a time there was a child who had strong and confusing feelings about many things. No one could actually share their feelings and they could not express them intelligently. Then someone helped them to use words faithfully and clearly to express themselves and understand their feelings. When the subjective feelings had an objective partner in stable words, they became less disturbing and controlling and more enjoyable and useful. A marriage between mysterious feelings and clarifying words produces a child of peace for us. We can choose our words while we do not choose our emotions.

Thursday

A Word is Worth 1000 Pictures

Pictures, whether photographs, drawings, paintings, sculptures or other images usually have words added to them as titles or descriptions. Words sometimes, but not usually, have images added to them. Images seem to need words more than words need images. Words stand alone. Words can be understood in different ways but don't need images to define them or add to their meaning. "In the beginning was the Word", not the image. Humans are in God's image partly because we can speak and be committed to our words. Let's treasure and be responsible for our words.

Friday

Life Is Hard

Natural life is given to us at conception. Eternal life is given to us when we believe in Jesus. Natural life will end in death. Natural life has a tremendous pull on us. It is easy to be natural – we only need to go with the flow and "be natural". This leads to death and is an easy slide. True life in Christ is a battle against death and is an active walk or run or fight. Choosing life is active and committed and needs God's help. Choosing death is passive. Life is hard. Death is easy.

Week Forty Seven

Monday

Believe and be Baptized

Water baptism is an obedient celebration of believing in Jesus and being baptized by His Spirit. The Bible teaches us to believe and repent and be baptized. The right order is to believe and be baptized, not to be baptized and maybe believe later. Being baptized does not save us. It celebrates and demonstrates our salvation. Water baptism can be controlled by the Church. Baptism by the Holy Spirit cannot be. Immersion shows our death and resurrection with Jesus. Sprinkling shows washing. Baptism should be done for anyone who believes in Jesus and asks for baptism.

Tuesday

Broken

We all experience a lot of broken things in life – broken bones, broken promises, broken hopes, broken marriages, broken careers. Our circumstances are all differently and variously broken. What we have in common is broken hearts or identities. Our most fundamental need is for Jesus to repair our broken hearts using His own Blood for glue. When our hearts are healed by Jesus and we have a new identity in Him, none of the other broken things can destroy us. Don't deny or run from your brokenness. Bring it to Jesus for healing. His Love for you is powerful.

Wednesday

Entitlements, Rights and Grace

Entitlements are created and granted by governments and institutions. Rights are imagined and guaranteed by the United Nations and other organizations. Grace is the gift of life to those who are not entitled and have no right to it. God gives the right to become His children to those who are not entitled to it. Many people have basic needs that are not met. They are not entitled to have those needs met. We are called by a gracious God to graciously help those in need, not because they deserve it but because God is Love.

Thursday

How Do You Know That?

We know things in different ways. How do you know you like chocolate? You know by experience. How do you know that two plus two equals four? You know by logic. How do you know to stop at the red light and go at the green light? You know by culture or institution or tradition. How do you know that Jesus loves you? You know by revelation from the eternal supernatural into space and time (the Bible tells me so). We need all these ways of knowing to know as God wants us to know.

Friday

Rejoicing in Suffering and Sorrow

Some of the events in the book of Revelation take place on earth and some in heaven (the supernatural dimensions of reality). The ones on earth take place in time, while the ones in heaven take place in eternity. "A day is like a thousand years and a thousand years is like a day" describes the relationship between time and eternity. Can we expect to measure the events in heaven with a calendar? Probably not. The events are true and real even though we cannot fully imagine or measure them. We live by faith and not by sight.

Week Forty Eight

Monday

Givers and Takers

Here are some questions concerning whether you are a giver or a taker. Do you ask how a Church can be a blessing to you or how you can be a blessing in the Church? Do you focus more on your rights or your responsibilities. Are you part of the problem or part of the solution? Think and pray for clarity about these things. Dare to ask others how they see you. Pray and work to be a giver and part of the solution. We know God will help you because this is what He wants for you.

Tuesday

Good Sermons

The sermon of Peter at Pentecost is a good model. A sermon should proclaim Christ and invite people to believe in Him. It should explain Scripture and connect the Old and New Testaments. It should comfort those who need comforting and rebuke those whose behavior is unchristian. It should tell stories to illustrate its points. It should apply Scripture to contemporary life and teach people how to live and think as followers of Jesus. This kind of message is good, rich and nourishing food. If you are a preacher, preach like this to bless your people.

Wednesday

Holy Creation

Holy means complete (wholly) and separate from everything that is incomplete. In Greek numerology, 7 represents completeness. 3 represents the trinitarian Creator and 4 represents the creation with 4 directions and 4 seasons. 777 represents trinitarian completeness or Holy, Holy, Holy. 666 represents "almost" or "counterfeit" or evil. God expressed Himself in the creation, which He said was very good or Wholly/Holy. The sin of rebellion by the devil and people separated the creation from the Creator and distorted it. God loves the creation and will make it holy again so we can live in it with Him.

Thursday

Ocean

In Mesopotamian myth Ocean controlled chaos; creating, surrounding and containing earth and sea. Also called serpent it gives birth to dragons. In the temple of Solomon, the Sea was the largest and only asymmetrical object. It was absurdly impractical as a washing vessel. The sea or Ocean is entirely contained and controlled by the temple or Kingdom of God. In Ezekiel's very detailed vision of the Temple the sea is not mentioned and in Revelation the sea is said to be no more. God is greater than all people's myths and imaginations and swallows them up in victorious control.

Friday

Information

Information is mysterious. We don't know exactly what it is, but no one doubts that it exists. Information controls matter, particularly genetic material, but there is no evidence that matter produces information. Materialists have faith that matter produces information. It is more likely that information is super-natural, coming from God, who holds every-thing together by the power of His Word. In the beginning was the Word. In the beginning was information. The Word became flesh and lived with us. We don't understand this, but we can be thankful and trust in this Truth. It is the best explanation for every-thing.

Week Forty Nine

Monday

Civil Disobedience

Civil disobedience is an option in the Chris-tian life, but it is questionable and needs careful clarity. Praying for those in authority over us is commanded and not questionable ever. In any situation we can be militantly active in praying and informing those in authority that we are supporting them in that way. Civil disobedience is sometimes appropriate. It is always appropriate to take a stand for God by asking Him to take a stand for us. Praying can lead and guide our actions. Acting instead of praying is always a mistake. Prioritize prayer and blessing the city.

Tuesday

Holy

In the Bible the basic meaning of Holy is separate or whole. God is whole or complete in Himself and separate from everything incomplete or distorted. He is Holy, Holy, Holy because He is three Persons. A thing or place is holy because it is set apart for God, belonging to Him and separate from the surrounding distortions. People are and become increasingly holy because they become one with Christ and each other, separate from the distortion and death of sin. We become holy by increasing in the fruits of the Holy Spirit. Be holy because God is Holy.

Wednesday

Humpty Dumpty

Humpty Dumpty is an egg in Alice in Wonderland, symbolizing all of us. He fell off a wall (it doesn't matter which side), smashed and died. Lewis Carroll tells us that all the King's horses and all the King's men couldn't put Humpty together again. But the King (Jesus) could. Jesus uses His own Blood to glue Humpty (all of us) together and give new life. Everyone, including children, can understand the Gospel in this story. We all need to be put together again. Admit your need and let Jesus put you together again in a new life.

Thursday

Innocent Victims

Everyone is innocent of something. Someone who is guilty of murder might be innocent of cruelty to dogs and tax evasion. We are all guilty of rebelling against God and distorting His Image. So, we all deserve death. If I am not deserving of being bullied but am deserving of death, which is worse? No one can completely protect us from being bullied. God can protect us from death through Jesus Christ. If someone is innocent of deserving being bullied but guilty of deserving death, which is the most important problem for them? Let's put first things first.

Friday

Love Your Enemies

Sometimes some people are our enemies. Sometimes we only perceive them as enemies. This perception produces anxiety, vindictiveness and negativity of many kinds, which are unhealthy in every way. Jesus taught us to love our enemies. We pray for people from a position of strength, asking God to bless them. If God does bless them, they will become less of an enemy to us. Instead of threatening enemies they become objects of mercy for us. This is a blessing for us and makes us strong in the Lord for good. Love and pray for your enemies.

Week Fifty

Monday

Our Achievements and God's

Many people look back and ask what they have achieved or accomplished in their lives. We should do what we can. What we do is individual and optional. What God does in us is general and essential. God works in us to change and shape us in our attitudes and motivations. We work to make and to do. If we accomplish much but don't let God work in us, we will be losers. If we accomplish little and let God work in us, we will be winners. Maximize both. Lean primarily on Jesus and His Work.

Tuesday

Patience

Patience is a fruit of the Spirit. It isn't usually a natural feature of people. Patience is part of the passive part of life. We need patience with other people and with God. Patience requires trust. Other people are not trustworthy, but we can be patient with them because we trust God. It is spiritually healthy to connect patience with humility rather than being proud of our patience. Patience feels like death because we die to our felt rights and needs. It is in dying to ourselves that we live in Christ. Patience is actually long term realism.

Wednesday

Real Life

Authenticating ourselves and living our best life does not establish our identities and make us secure and real. It only puts us at the center of reality so that we get crushed. Reality and security only come from Jesus Christ. Affirming and approving each other feels good and seems real but only the affirmation and approval of Jesus are good and real. We can encourage and support each other without playing God with each other. We don't make reality by imagining it. Let Jesus make you real. Jesus paid for your life. Accept it from Him on His terms.

Thursday

Amen

"Amen" is a Hebrew word meaning "yes" or "agreed". When we pray with others we say "Amen" when we agree with a prayer and don't say "Amen" if we disagree or are not sure. When we pray alone "Amen" is like a signature at the end of a letter. When others pray or make statements, saying "Amen" is like signing their letter. Saying "Amen" should not be automatic or thoughtless. Amen does not mean "uh-huh" or "whatever". It means "yes". We are responsible before God to listen carefully to what people say or pray and agree or not agree.

Friday

Row, Row, Row your Boat

Row, row, row your boat gently down the stream.
Merrily, merrily, merrily, merrily life is but a dream.

Many people know this song and love to sing it as a round. We should not stop singing together but should also be aware that the song expresses a nihilistic worldview and is a dark joke. Boats are mostly rowed upstream and coast downstream. If life is only a dream, is there an actual reality?

Consider this translation:
Propel, propel, propel your craft serenely down the solution.
Extatically, extatically, extatically, extatically, existence is but an illusion.

Week Fifty One

Monday

Sexual Liberation

In our Western culture it is normal and acceptable for men to say they want or need a wife. Meanwhile it is shameful gender disloyalty for women to say they want or need a husband. Some questions suggest themselves: Do men need wives, while women do not need husbands? If the need is equal, why are women suppressed in their expression of it? Do men impose this oppression on women or do women impose it on each other? Are women victims of their liberation? How can we work for more equality in this area of sexual freedom?

Tuesday

Sheep and Goats

Sheep are clumsy, dependent, easily disoriented and tend to get lost. Goats are sure footed, independent, well oriented and self-sufficient. It is not a compliment to be called a sheep. Many people would like to be a goat for God. G.O.A.T.s (the greatest of all time) are proud. Being a sheep requires poverty of spirit – the first principle of entering the Kingdom of God according to the Sermon on the Mount. Be a sheep for God. Be totally dependent on Jesus, His Word in Scripture and the Holy Spirit. Jesus keeps the sheep and sends goats away.

Wednesday

Systemic Racism

Systemic means throughout the system. In a national system, systemic racism means segregation or persecution required or permitted by law. Racism can be a real problem without being systemic. In all countries sin and pride are systemic. In some countries abortion and adultery are systemic. In some countries religious prejudice is systemic. Smaller systems like Churches or clubs can be systematically racist by rules or pervasive attitude. Saying that racism is systemic can be a cultural and political exaggeration used to shape our thinking unrealistically. Political and advertising slogans seduce us. Stay awake, be responsible and test everything.

Thursday

Testimonies

A testimony (from "testa" – head) is a declaration or witness of what is known to be true. The law in the Old Testament is testimony of what is true about God and obeying Him. A testimony about Jesus is a statement of what is true about Jesus. A Biblical testimony is not about myself or my experiences. It is important for Christians to give testimony about Jesus to each other for clarification, unification and discussion. In this way our knowledge about Jesus is stabilized, deepened and expanded. We should give testimonies without using "I", "me" or "mine" in them.

Friday

The Circle and the Cross

The circle is a symbol of unity and perfection. It is used in various philosophies and religions. It has an inside and an outside. How do we get inside? A circle is necessarily concentric or self-centered. It doesn't work as a symbol for Christianity. The symbol of Christianity is the Cross. The Cross is basically human in shape. It is radiant and embracing. It is a symbol of love, sacrifice, invitation, acceptance and victory of good over evil and truth over falsehood. It is a mystery that can be realized fully by living, not only by understanding.

Week Fifty Two

Monday

Blasphemy

Cursing or using God's name in stupid ways is not good. As a habit they are destructive infections in our language. Blasphemy has the deeper and more subtle meaning of using God's name or character for our own vanity. If we say "God said or told me" about what we imagine or hope it can be like signing God's Name to something we make up. This is forgery and can be manipulative. We create God in the image of our own imagination. Blasphemy is false prophecy that creates confusion about God in the community of His People. Avoid blasphemy.

Tuesday

The Rock

God is our Rock. We can stand on Him. He is solid and dependable, sustaining, and necessary. Jesus is our Rock, the cornerstone of the building of the Church family. Water came out of the Rock to refresh the people. Water came out of Jesus when He was punished for us. We can choose to build our lives and relationships on the Rock or it will fall on us and crush us. The stones cry out for the Rock Who made them. By believing and declaring that Jesus Christ is the Rock, Peter and we become Christian or "Rockian".

Wednesday

To Be or Not to Be Vaccinated

Concerning the issue of being vaccinated or not, a question that applies in many situations is relevant here: "Am I being part of the problem or part of the solution?" "Solution" means moving toward getting rid of the masks, segregation and lack of trust we are experiencing now. People who are not vaccinated have an advantage over those who are vaccinated: the unvaccinated have the possibility of changing their minds, while the vaccinated do not. May God bless us all and move us to love and pray for each other. Amen.

Thursday

Victim or Criminal?

We are all victims in various ways. The weather, the economy, disease, accident, war, crime, depression and enemies all victimize us and make us suffer. We need salvation, deliverance and protection from all these things. What we most deeply need salvation from is not what happens to us but what we do; whether we trust and obey God, whether we accept life and identity from God or try to make it out of our own imagination and desire. We don't need a repair job. We have destroyed ourselves and need to be remade. Repent and be saved.

Friday

Weakness and Courage

Courage is naturally associated with strength. The superhero has courage because of special abilities. Courage is not using our strength and confidence but acting when we are weak and afraid. When we pray for help and trust in God, we experience supernatural power to love, care, serve and speak God's Truth. The more often we do this the more we see God's power making our weak efforts complete and effective, even beyond our imagination. Eventually, like the Apostle Paul, we come to rejoice in our weaknesses because through them we experience God's power for good and life.

www.ingramcontent.com/pod-product-compliance
Lightning Source LLC
Chambersburg PA
CBHW070128080526
44586CB00015B/1603